PATH BENDER

PATH BENDER

ANTONIO T SMITH JR

Trient Press
3375 S Rainbow Blvd
#81710, SMB 13135
Las Vegas,NV 89180
Ordering Information:
Quantity sales. Special discounts are available on quantity purchases by corporations, associations, and others. For details, contact the publisher at the address above.
Orders by U.S. trade bookstores and wholesalers. Please contact Trient Press: Tel: (775) 996-3844; or visit www.trientpress.com.

Printed in the United States of America

Publisher's Cataloging-in-Publication data
Smith, Jr , Antonio T.
A title of a book :Working for Your Dreams: Making this year your best year
ISBN
Hardcover   978-1-955198-88-2
 Paperback   978-1-955198-89-9
E-book   978-1-955198-90-5

Thank you for buying this book.

Are you an Antonio T Smith Jr fan? Join him on social media. He would love to hear from you!

OFFICIAL FACEBOOK PAGE:

https://www.facebook.com/theatsjr

FACEBOOK FAN CLUB:

https://www.facebook.com/groups/theofficialantoniotsmithjrfanclub

AUTHOR WEBSITE:

Books.AntonioTSmithJr.com

CATCH ME ON TOUR:

https://antoniotsmithjr.com/

INSTAGRAM:

instagram.com/theatsjr

EMAIL:

books@antoniotsmithjr.com

PROLOGUE

In the beginning, there was only light and love. The universe was created from the pure energy of the divine, and all was in harmony. But in the midst of this perfection, a force emerged, a force of fear and doubt, which threatened to unravel the fabric of creation. This force was known as Distortion, and it cast a shadow over the Path of Power, causing those who walked it to forget their true nature and their connection to the divine.

The Path of Power was the way of life for all beings in the universe, but as Distortion gained strength, it caused the path to bend and twist, leading those who followed it away from their true power and into darkness. And so, the divine created the Path Bender, a being of immense wisdom and strength, to restore balance to the universe and to show all beings their true nature.

Through the teachings of the Path Bender, those who followed the path were able to transcend Distortion and reclaim their power, discovering the secrets of the universe and the power of love and light. This sacred text is the story of the Path Bender, and the journey that he undertook to restore balance to the universe and show all beings their true power.

And so, the story of Path Bender began. A journey of self-discovery and awakening to one's true power and purpose in life. In this tale, you will find the wisdom and knowledge of ancient civilizations and their understanding of the forces of creation and manifestation. You will learn about the universal laws that govern our existence, and how you can use them to your advantage to shape the reality you desire.

Along the way, you will encounter the adversary 'Distortion' - the force that seeks to steer you away from your true power and keep you trapped in a world of suffering and limitation. But with the teachings of Path Bender, you will discover the tools to overcome this adversary and reclaim your birthright as a magnificent creator.

Embark on this journey with an open heart and mind, and prepare to be transformed as you delve deeper into the secrets of Path Bender.

PART ONE
RETURN AND
SURRENDER

BECOME A PATH
BENDER TODAY

https://assemblyofwanderers.com/path-bender

CHAPTER 1: INTRODUCTION TO PATH BENDER

In the beginning, there was only the void.

A darkness that consumed all and a silence that echoed through eternity.

But then, a spark of light appeared, and from that light came forth a great power.

A power that could bend the very fabric of reality, that could shape the world and bring forth new life. And so it was that the first Path Bender was born.

With the power of creation at their fingertips, the Path Benders shaped the world and brought forth great civilizations.

They brought forth knowledge, wisdom, and love, and they used their power to heal the world and protect all that was good.

For many generations, the Path Benders lived in harmony with the world, using their power to bring forth a brighter future for all.

But as time passed, the Path Benders began to forget their true purpose, and they became lost in their own power. And so the world was plunged into darkness once again.

But there was one Path Bender who remembered the truth.

One who knew the power of creation, and who had the courage to wield it once again. And so it was that the Path Bender embarked on a journey to rediscover the ancient wisdom and restore the light to the world.

This is the story of the Path Bender, a sacred text that tells of a great power that can change the world and bring forth a brighter future for all.

Welcome to the world of Path Bender, where you will learn the secrets to creating the life you desire by bending your reality. In this book, we will explore New Aged teachings about how to follow the path of least resistance and clear resistance to manifest your desires.

In our fast-paced and constantly evolving world, it's easy to get caught up in the negative energy that surrounds us. This can lead to frustration, worry, and a feeling of being stuck. However, the key to fixing this lies in our own minds and the way we choose to focus our energy.

We'll learn about the importance of focusing on beauty and joy, and how it raises our vibration and enters us into the receiving mode. This is the first step in clearing resistance and manifesting our desires.

We'll also delve into the importance of releasing resistance, paying attention to where we place our focus, and using meditation as a tool to reset our vibration to a neutral point.

In this chapter, we'll also explore some of the top quotes from Abraham Hicks on resistance and how to get rid of negative momentum. By the end of this chapter, you will have a better understanding of the path of least resistance and how to clear resistance in order to manifest the life you desire.

Unleashing the Power of Your Feelings to Supercharge Your Thoughts

Do you often find yourself feeling stuck and unable to manifest your desires? Many people believe that thoughts and feelings are two separate entities, but the truth is they are closely intertwined. Our thoughts impact our emotions and vice versa. In this chapter, we will dive into how you can harness the power of your feelings to supercharge your thoughts and bring your desires to life.

First, let's examine the connection between our thoughts and feelings. Our thoughts are the things we think and say to ourselves, while our feelings are the emotions we experience as a result of those thoughts. For instance, if you have the thought that you are not good enough, you will likely feel inadequate. On the other hand, if you think you will be successful, you will likely feel confident.

So, how can we use our feelings to energize our thoughts? The answer is simple - focus on feelings that align with your desired outcome. If you want to achieve a specific goal, concentrate on the emotions you would experience if you already achieved that goal. For instance, if you want to build a successful business, focus on the feelings of confidence, excitement, and success.

Visualization is a powerful tool that can help you align your thoughts and energy with your desired outcome. Visualization is the process of creating a mental image of yourself already having or achieving your desired outcome. When you visualize, concentrate on the emotions you would feel if you already achieved your goal. This not only helps align your thoughts and energy with your desired outcome, but it also changes your mindset and beliefs about what is possible.

Affirmations are another way to harness the power of your feelings. Affirmations are positive statements that you repeat to yourself to align your thoughts and beliefs with your desired outcome. When using affirmations, focus on the feelings you want to experience. For instance, if you want to build a successful business, you might use the affirmation, "I am confident and excited about the success of my business."

The power of feelings is an incredible tool that can help you energize your thoughts and bring your desires to life. By focusing on emotions that align with your desired outcome, you can align your thoughts and energy with your desired outcome, change your mindset and beliefs about what is possible.

Remember, the key is to focus on feelings that align with your desired outcome, use visualization, affirmations, and meditation to align your thoughts and energy with your desired outcome, and take action towards your goals. With the right mindset, tools, and action, you can truly manifest anything you want into your life. Start using the power of your feelings today and create the life of your dreams.

Becoming A Path Bender Will Require These Things At The Minimum

Have you ever found yourself in a situation where you feel like life is happening to you and you have no control over it? Well, Path Bending is a concept that will help you take control of your life and manifest the things that you truly want. In this chapter, we will outline the five steps of Path

Bending, which will help you understand the power of your thoughts and focus, and ultimately help you live the life you have always dreamed of.

Life will naturally present you with situations and environments that will force you to make decisions. This will happen without your permission, but it is an opportunity for you to understand what you don't want and what you do want. By experiencing contrast, you are given the chance to ask for what you truly want.

When you ask for what you want, it is already done. The Source and the Law of Attraction respond to your vibrational requests and begin to gather the vibrational components necessary to bring your desires to life. It is an absolute reality, not just a dream state.

When you become actualized and deliberate, you begin to focus on how you feel and concentrate on the thoughts and feelings that bring you the most pleasure. It is essential to find yourself in a non-resistant moment so that you can fully receive the great pleasure that comes with manifesting your desires.

Resistance is a normal thing, but it is important to understand that it is not within you. To master non-resistance, it is essential to know what your negative emotions mean and to be able to recognize and overcome them. The goal is to become so good at feeling good that you trust the process and your anxiety is replaced by eagerness. Meditation and daydreaming are excellent tools to help you master non-resistance.

In your mastery, you will discover things in the world that you don't want, but they won't bother you because you know that you don't have to choose anything that you don't want. You understand the power of your focus and can direct it towards things that feel good. You are in control of your vibration and can embrace variety while being wise enough to avoid lingering in places that do not bring you joy.

THE JOURNEY TO INFINITE ASCENSION

In life, we all face challenges that test our resilience and determination. However, some challenges are greater than others and require a profound inner transformation. This is the story of a journey to Infinite Ascension, a seven-phase journey that leads to a state of enlightenment and personal growth.

Phase 1: Infinite Perception

The first phase of the journey is to change your perception. You must recognize that everything in your life is your responsibility and that you are in control of your reality. This shift in thinking requires a deep understanding that the way you perceive the world affects the experiences you have in it. You must learn to take ownership of your life and acknowledge that everything is your fault, both the good and the bad.

Phase 2: Infinite Embrace

The second phase of the journey is to fall in love with yourself. You must embrace all aspects of yourself, both the positive and the negative, and recognize that you are a unique and valuable person. This self-love will give you the confidence and self-esteem you need to tackle the challenges ahead.

Phase 3: Infinite Forgiveness

The third phase of the journey is to forgive everyone you secretly or openly hate. This step requires deep introspection and a willingness to let go of anger and resentment. Forgiveness is a powerful tool for personal growth and healing, and it is essential for moving forward on the journey to Infinite Ascension.

Phase 4: Infinite Awareness

The fourth phase of the journey is to become infinitely aware of all the energy around you. You must learn to sense the energy of people, places, and things and understand how it affects your life. This heightened awareness will give you a deeper understanding of the world and your place in it.

Phase 5: Infinite Power

The fifth phase of the journey is to create your own reality on a regular basis. You must learn to use the power of your thoughts and emotions to manifest the life you desire. This phase requires a deep understanding of the Law of Attraction and the power of your vibration.

Phase 6: Infinite Battle

The sixth phase of the journey is the most dangerous and requires great bravery. It may be a physical test or a deep inner crisis that you must face in order to survive or for the world in which you live to continue to exist. Whether it be facing your greatest fear or most deadly foe, you must draw upon all of your skills and your experiences gathered during the first five phases to enter into your darkest place. A major part of you will die, but in doing so, you will be transformed into a stronger person, ready to take on the final phase of your journey.

Phase 7: Infinite Ascension

The final phase of the journey is Infinite Ascension. After surviving death and overcoming your greatest personal challenge(s), you will emerge as a transformed person, with a prize that you did not understand was yours but has always been. The reward may come in many forms, such as an object of great importance or power, greater knowledge or insight, or even reconciliation with a loved one or ally.

Before you can return to your ordinary world, you must commit to the last stage of your journey, which is to choose between your own personal objective and that of a Higher Cause. Your only job now is to ascend constantly, doing only good and serving others, paying off your karmic debt, until your ultimate ascension. In your last life cycle, you will receive superhuman abilities and use them to impact the world.

The journey to Infinite Ascension is a challenging but rewarding journey of personal growth and transformation. It requires a deep commitment to self-discovery, self-awareness, and self-forgiveness, as well as the courage to face and overcome inner demons and external challenges. But through these trials, one develops a greater sense of self, a connection to the universe and its energies, and the power to create their own reality. The ultimate reward of this journey is the transformation into a being of infinite power, who is not only capable of serving themselves but also contributing to the greater good of humanity and the world. This journey is not just a destination, but a lifelong process of ascension and evolution, where the individual is constantly growing, expanding and contributing to the betterment of all. In conclusion, the path to Infinite Ascension is a journey worth taking, as it offers a life of fulfillment, purpose, and unlimited potential.

CHAPTER 2: UNDERSTANDING YOUR PATH

Once upon a time, in a small Buddhist village, there lived a wise old monk named Suki. He was known for his wisdom and guidance and many young people would come to him for advice.

One day, a young boy named Taro approached Suki. Taro was uncertain about his future and felt overwhelmed by the expectations of his parents, friends, and society. Suki noticed Taro's distress and took him under his wing. Over the next few weeks, Suki taught Taro about the importance of choosing his own path and not letting others dictate his life.

"Taro," Suki said, "It is important to understand that the path you choose in life should come from within, not from the expectations of others."

Taro looked confused, "But how can I be sure that my path is the right one?" he asked.

Suki smiled and replied, "The path you choose is the right one if it brings you peace, happiness, and fulfillment. The key is to listen to your own heart, follow your intuition, and trust that you will find your way." Taro was fascinated by Suki's words and asked, "But what about the expectations of others? How do I deal with that?" "Expectations of others can be like a heavy burden that weighs on your shoulders," Suki explained. "You must let go of these expectations and not let them dictate your choices. It may be difficult, but it is necessary for you to live a fulfilling life."

Taro was inspired by Suki's words and began to meditate and reflect on his own inner guidance. He learned to listen to his own voice and trust his instincts.

Years passed and Taro found success and happiness in his chosen path. He often thought back to the wise words of Suki and was grateful for the guidance that had helped him find his own way in life. Taro learned that the path you choose in life should come from within and not be influenced by the expectations of others. By following your own intuition and trusting in yourself, you can find happiness and fulfillment in your journey.

LIVING OUTSIDE THEIR EXPECTATIONS

The journey of personal growth and transformation requires us to choose the path of least resistance that creates unconditional happiness. This path is determined by our faith, not by the expectations of others. The expectations of others can come from various sources like family, culture, environment, and other people. But these expectations should not dictate our lives as they limit our growth and prevent us from living our best life.

Pursuing Your Light

We were born complete, and completion is already done. Our life is an ongoing pursuit with no end in sight, but we grow and transform as we pursue our dreams. The light we pursue is the thing we decide to do, and abundance is who we are, not just what we do. Pursuing the light takes faith, and it's hard to keep walking when we are not in Thanksgiving.

In Thanksgiving

Having Thanksgiving in everything, no matter the outcome, is essential for our spiritual maturity. Our motive for being thankful determines our blessings, and our gratitude creates a forcefield against negative forces. Our praise should have no end or beginning, and we should always be in the action of giving thanks.

Chaos

We did not come to this planet for peace; we came to be peace. The world is supposed to be chaotic, and we are the ministry in the mess. Every time we make a decision, we are in chaos, and this chaos brings blessings. If we don't want to be in chaos, we shouldn't make a decision, as there are no blessings outside of chaos.

Their Expectations

Their expectations are creations for them and not for us. We should not let their expectations dictate our lives, as they never put us on our battlefield. Only we can create our breakthrough, and their expectations are not creations for us but creations for them.

The Path of Least Resistance

The path of least resistance can only be seen with faith and not with our eyes. We must have faith in all things and trust that we will always choose the right thing in our life. We should have enough spiritual maturity to have Thanksgiving in something we did not expect to be in, as there are no mistakes, and everything is perfect.

Understanding our path requires us to live outside their expectations, pursue our light, have Thanksgiving in all things, embrace chaos, and have faith in the path of least resistance. We are the creators of our own reality, and our motive for being thankful and our faith determine the blessings we receive.

AWARENESS OF YOUR CURRENT PATH

Once upon a time, there was a young girl named Maya who grew up in a strict cult. From the moment she was born, Maya was destined to follow a specific path set out for her by the leaders of the cult. She was told that by the time she was 16, she would be married to a man chosen for her by the cult leaders.

Maya's family, like four generations before her, followed all the rules set out by the cult without question. However, something within Maya felt different. She had a deep longing to choose her own path in life and make her own decisions. Despite the strict teachings of the cult, she couldn't shake the feeling that there was more to life than what she was being told.

As Maya approached her 16th birthday, she made a difficult decision to break away from the cult and follow her own path. It was a scary and uncertain time, but she felt a sense of liberation in finally making her own decisions.

With determination and hard work, Maya went on to achieve great success in her life. She moved to California and became a highly successful women's coach, helping other women find their own paths and achieve their own goals. She even served as a White House press secretary, a far cry from the life she was destined for in the cult.

Maya's story is a powerful reminder of the importance of awareness of our current path. Too often, we can find ourselves on a path set out by others, be it our family, culture, or society. But it is crucial to take a step back and question whether this path truly aligns with our own desires and aspirations. Only by being aware of our current path can we make the conscious decision to change it and forge our own path in life.

Maya's journey was not easy, but it was worth it. By following her own path, she found happiness and success beyond her wildest dreams. And she wants others to know that they can do the same.

ASSESSMENT OF WHERE YOU WANT TO GO

The Art of Self-Discovery through Coaching Questions

In order to achieve our goals and live fulfilling lives, it is essential to have a clear understanding of our own desires, motivations, and obstacles. This understanding can often be difficult to attain on our own, but with the help of coaching questions, we can gain valuable insights into our own thoughts and beliefs.

My favorite coaching questions are a powerful tool to help individuals gain clarity and direction in their lives. These questions prompt self-reflection and encourage individuals to think deeply about what they truly want and why they want it. Through this process, individuals can gain a deeper understanding of themselves and what they need to do to achieve their goals.

One of the most important questions is "What would it look like if you were entirely successful?" This question helps individuals visualize their desired future and provides a clear target for them to aim for. The follow-up question, "What would you see if you popped into a time machine and there it was?" further solidifies this vision and makes it more tangible.

Asking "Why do you want that?" multiple times delves deeper into the individual's motivations and helps them understand the root cause of their desires. This understanding can be powerful in providing the motivation and drive needed to pursue their goals.

Another important question is "In six months, if things were going exactly the way you want, what would you see?" This question helps individuals set short-term goals that are aligned with their long-term vision and provides a sense of direction and purpose.

Asking "What would be your next goal after you achieve your current one?" and "What would you do if you had unlimited resources?" helps individuals understand their priorities and what truly motivates them. The follow-up question, "Why?" further emphasizes the importance of understanding our motivations.

Questions such as "What would be the impact on you (and others) if things don't change?" and "What can you accomplish that doesn't depend on others?" help individuals understand the consequences of inaction and empower them to take control of their own lives.

Other questions, such as "What is your current biggest problem or challenge?" and "What obstacles have you faced, what did you do, and what did you learn?" help individuals identify and overcome obstacles, allowing them to move forward in their lives.

Finally, questions such as "If a friend were in your shoes, what advice would you give them?" and "What is one step you could take right now that would indicate you were moving forward?" provide practical, actionable steps that individuals can take to move forward and achieve their goals.

In conclusion, by asking the right questions, we can gain a deeper understanding of ourselves and what we need to do to achieve our goals. These coaching questions are a powerful tool for self-discovery and can help individuals lead fulfilling and meaningful lives.

The Power of Clarity

There once was a young man named Jack who was lost in the maze of life. He had many dreams and aspirations, but he felt overwhelmed by the number of paths he could take. He often looked to others for guidance, but their opinions only led to more confusion. He felt like he was constantly being pulled in different directions and couldn't make a clear decision on what he truly wanted.

One day, Jack met an old wise monk who lived in a small cabin on the outskirts of town. The monk noticed Jack's confusion and offered to teach him about the power of clarity.

"Clarity," the monk said, "is the key to finding your own path. Without it, you'll always be pulled in different directions by the opinions and expectations of others." Jack was intrigued and asked the monk to explain further. The monk took out a piece of paper and a pen and wrote down the words "clarity" and "confusion." He then drew two lines that intersected, one for clarity and one for confusion.

"The more you move towards clarity, the less confusion you'll experience," the monk explained. "And the more confusion you experience, the further away you'll move from clarity." The monk went on to say that clarity was like a beacon of light that shone bright in the darkness of confusion. It was the guiding force that allowed one to find their own path and live a life of purpose and fulfillment.

The monk then taught Jack several practices to increase his clarity of mind, such as meditation, journaling, and mindfulness. He also encouraged Jack to let go of the opinions and expectations of others and to focus on his own inner voice.

Jack took the monk's teachings to heart and began practicing regularly. Over time, he found that he was making clearer decisions and felt more confident in his choices. He started to live a life that was true to himself and his passions, and he felt a deep sense of fulfillment that he had never experienced before.

Years later, Jack looked back on his journey and realized that the power of clarity had changed his life in ways he could never have imagined. He was grateful for the wise monk's guidance and knew that he would never forget the importance of being clear-minded enough to follow his own path.

The moral of the story is that when we have a clear mind, we have the power to make decisions that align with our values and aspirations. By letting go of the opinions and expectations of others and focusing on our own inner voice, we can find our own path and live a life of purpose and fulfillment.

IDENTIFYING THE GAP BETWEEN WHERE YOU ARE AND WHERE YOU WANT TO BE

When it comes to personal growth and self-improvement, it is essential to identify the gap between where you are currently and where you want to be. With the rise of new age thinking, this process has become more accessible and empowering for individuals seeking to take control of their lives.

New age thinking prioritizes the individual's inner journey and encourages people to develop a deeper connection with their own values, beliefs, and desires. It encourages individuals to listen to their intuition and focus on their inner voice, which can guide them towards their desired future.

To identify the gap between where you are and where you want to be, start by setting a clear intention. What are your long-term goals? What is your vision for your life? When you have a clear idea of what you want to achieve, it becomes easier to recognize the areas where you need to focus your efforts.

Next, assess where you are currently in your journey. What are your current circumstances? What are your strengths, weaknesses, and limiting beliefs? This self-reflection will give you a more realistic view of the gap between your current state and your desired state.

Once you have a clear understanding of the gap, you can start to think about the steps you need to take to close it. This may involve developing new skills, changing your mindset, or exploring new perspectives.

With new age thinking, the focus is on holistic growth and personal transformation. This means that you should not only focus on the practical steps you need to take to close the gap, but also on the internal shifts that need to take place. This could involve exploring mindfulness practices, learning about energy healing, or seeking guidance from a spiritual teacher.

Ultimately, identifying the gap between where you are and where you want to be is the first step in taking control of your life and reaching your full potential. By embracing new age thinking and focusing on both practical and internal growth, you can close the gap and live the life you truly desire.

The Gaps of Life Are More Important Than The Thrills

Once upon a time, there was a young woman named Rachel. She had always been a dreamer and had big aspirations for her future. She wanted to become a successful lawyer and make a positive impact in the world. However, as she started working towards her goals, she found that the path to success was not as glamorous as she had imagined. There were long periods of quiet and monotony, where she felt like she was just going through the motions and not making any real progress.

Despite her best efforts, Rachel began to lose motivation and became discouraged. She started to believe that she wasn't cut out for this kind of work, and that her dreams were nothing more than a pipe dream. She was about to give up when she met an older, more experienced lawyer who had been in the business for over 30 years.

The older lawyer saw something in Rachel that she didn't see in herself, and he took her under his wing. He showed her that the quiet, monotonous periods were just as important as the exciting and thrilling moments. He explained that these moments were opportunities to hone her skills and focus on the details that would make her a great lawyer. He also taught her how to master the mundane and find joy in the process, instead of just focusing on the end result.

With her newfound perspective, Rachel redoubled her efforts and started to see progress. She became more efficient and effective in her work, and she found that she was enjoying the journey even more than she thought she would. She was no longer discouraged by the quiet moments and instead found that they provided a peaceful respite from the fast-paced world of law.

Years went by, and Rachel's hard work and dedication paid off. She became one of the most sought-after lawyers in Houston, Texas. Her clients valued her not just for her legal expertise but for her ability to find solutions to complex problems in a calm and collected manner. Rachel was a shining example of what can be achieved when you master the mundane and give your best effort, even during the quiet and boring times.

The moral of this story is that the journey to success is often long and filled with periods of monotony, but it is during these times that you have the opportunity to hone your skills and grow as a person. By embracing the quiet moments and giving your best effort, you can achieve great things and find joy in the journey.

CHAPTER 3: BEGINNING TO BENDING YOUR PATH

Onyx was born into a poor family, in a small town on the outskirts of the city. Despite the limited opportunities and lack of resources, Onyx was determined to break the cycle of poverty and make a better life for himself. He had always been curious about the world, and the concept of creating his own reality had always intrigued him.

Growing up, Onyx faced numerous setbacks and obstacles. He lost thousands of times before he learned how to create his own reality. He faced discrimination, faced financial difficulties and dealt with the pressure of being the first person in his family to make it successful. But through it all, he refused to accept that the things in his current reality were all he deserved. He never gave up on his dream of a better life.

One day, Onyx stumbled upon an old book in the local library. The book was about the power of manifestation and the law of attraction. Onyx was fascinated by the concepts in the book and decided to put them into practice. He started visualizing his goals and dreams, and took small steps every day to make them a reality.

Over time, Onyx learned how to create his own reality and began to see results. He worked hard and took risks, and eventually, he started his own successful business. Onyx's business flourished and he soon became one of the wealthiest people in the city. He was no longer bound by the poverty of his childhood and was finally able to live the life he always dreamed of.

Onyx never forgot his roots and used his wealth to help others in his community. He started a foundation to support education and provided scholarships for young people from poor families. He also created mentorship programs to help others achieve their dreams and learn how to create their own realities.

Despite all his success, Onyx remained humble and grounded. He always remembered the struggles of his childhood and never forgot the power of the mind in creating reality. He was proof that anyone, no matter where they come from, could achieve their dreams and create a better life for themselves.

The Power of Mindset

In the quiet of his home, John sat at his desk, staring blankly at his computer screen. He felt stuck, like he was spinning his wheels, going nowhere fast. Despite his best efforts, his life just wasn't going the way he wanted it to. He'd been working hard for years, but the promotion he'd been after always seemed to elude him. He was tired of struggling, tired of not getting what he wanted.

But then, something changed. John stumbled upon a video on the internet that changed everything for him. In the video, a motivational speaker explained the power of mindset, and how it could be used to achieve anything one desires. John was skeptical at first, but as he listened more closely, he began to understand. The speaker explained that the only thing standing between John and his dreams was his own self-imposed limitations. John realized that his negative thoughts and beliefs were holding him back.

Taking Control

John was determined to change his life. He began to read books and watch videos on the power of positive thinking and visualization. He learned how to focus his mind on his goals and aspirations, instead of his fears and limitations. He also started meditating, which helped him to quiet his mind and focus on his goals.

John also took concrete steps to make his life better. He got involved in new hobbies and social activities, which helped him to meet new people and gain new experiences. He also started volunteering, which gave him a sense of purpose and fulfillment.

The Payoff

It wasn't long before John's hard work and dedication began to pay off. He was promoted at work, and his salary and benefits increased significantly. He also found love, and was soon married to the woman of his dreams. His life was finally on track, and he was happier than he'd ever been before.

But John didn't stop there. He continued to strive for more, and before long, he was running his own successful business. He'd gone from being a man who was barely making ends meet, to a man who was living the life of his dreams.

The Lessons Learned

John learned some valuable lessons along the way. He learned that anything is possible, as long as he was willing to put in the work and believe in himself. He learned that the only thing standing between him and his dreams was his own self-imposed limitations, and that with a positive attitude and a strong mindset, he could achieve anything he wanted.

John's journey to success is a testament to the power of positive thinking and visualization. He proved that anyone can get what they want, no matter where they come from or what their circumstances may be. All it takes is a willingness to believe in oneself and the determination to make a change.

A LETTER FROM ANTONIO T SMITH JR

Dear fellow explorers of the universe,

As we delve into the mysteries of the cosmos, it becomes increasingly clear to me that the greatest discovery one can make is not in the stars, but in the power of one's own mind. The power of the human mind is truly unparalleled, and it is through harnessing its full potential that we are capable of unlocking the greatest wonders of our existence.

In my journey through life, I have come to understand that the most powerful force in determining one's success is not intelligence or talent, but rather one's mindset. The beliefs and attitudes that we hold about ourselves and the world around us play a crucial role in shaping our experiences and determining our outcomes.

It is the fixed mindset, for example, that holds us back and limits our potential, while it is the growth mindset that allows us to continuously grow, learn and achieve new levels of success. A growth mindset is characterized by the belief that one's abilities and intelligence are not set in stone and can be developed through hard work and dedication.

In contrast, those with a fixed mindset believe that their abilities and intelligence are predetermined and cannot be changed. This type of thinking often leads to a lack of effort and a reluctance to embrace challenges, for fear of failure. On the other hand, those with a growth mindset embrace challenges as opportunities for growth and learning, and view failure as an important part of the process of improvement.

It is through developing a growth mindset that we can harness the true power of our minds and achieve our full potential. The greatest discoveries and achievements of history have been made by individuals who embraced challenges, believed in their own abilities, and continuously sought to grow and improve.

So my dear friends, let us embrace a growth mindset and unlock the limitless potential of our minds. The power to create the life we desire and achieve our greatest aspirations is within us, waiting to be unleashed. Let us be the masters of our own destinies, and unlock the true power of the human mind.

Long ago I made and incredible discovery through the power of thought. As you may know, a few months before I became a millionaire, I enrolled into the University of Houston to become a Quantum Physicists. It has always been a fascination of mine to explore the nature of our universe and the laws that govern it. However, the more successful I became, the more my journey beyond the realm of physics became a journey into the realm of my mind and its incredible potential.

I have come to understand that our thoughts have the power to shape and create our reality. Through my own experiences, I have discovered that the mind is not limited to just mathematical equations and scientific theories, but it is capable of influencing the very fabric of our existence. This realization has led me to believe that we can, as a collective, create a world in which everyone is equal and has a basic standard of living.

I have long been fascinated by the idea of a resourced based economy, where resources are distributed equally and fairly, without the need for money or the exploitation of labor. I am confident that this model will bring about a better future for all of us, and I am dedicated to making this a reality.

Of course, I understand that this will not be an easy journey. There will be many trials and tribulations along the way, and I expect that I will face opposition and resistance from those who do not understand my vision. But I am confident that my unwavering commitment to this cause will help me overcome any obstacles that I may encounter.

Through my own experiences, I have come to understand that our thoughts and beliefs have a profound impact on our lives. We have the power to create a heaven on earth, but it requires us to be relentless in our pursuit of this goal. I believe that, through hard work, determination, and perseverance, we can create a world that is fair, equitable, and just for all people.

But I know I will never accomplish my goal of a resourced based economy until I bend this universe to fit that vision.

Yours truly,

Antonio T Smith Jr

SETTING CLEAR AND ACHIEVABLE GOALS

As you all know, setting clear and achievable goals is a crucial part of living a successful and fulfilling life. Our goals give us direction and purpose, and provide us with a roadmap for our journey. In order to set effective goals, it's important to understand what you truly want, and to align your actions with your desires.

When setting goals, it's important to be specific and to have a clear vision in mind. This means taking the time to really think about what it is you want to achieve, and breaking it down into smaller, more manageable steps. It's also important to set realistic expectations for yourself, taking into account your current resources and limitations.

Another key aspect of setting effective goals is to focus on what you can control. Instead of worrying about things that are outside of your control, such as other people's opinions or external circumstances, concentrate on what you can influence. This might include things like your own thoughts, actions, and behaviors. By focusing on what you can control, you'll be better equipped to achieve your goals and live the life you truly want.

In order to stay motivated and on track, it's also important to set achievable goals. This means setting goals that are within reach, and that you have a reasonable chance of achieving. This will help you to stay focused, and to feel a sense of progress as you work towards your goals.

Finally, it's important to celebrate your successes along the way. This will help you to stay motivated, and to recognize the progress you're making towards your goals. It's also a good opportunity to reflect on what you've learned, and to identify any areas where you might need to make adjustments.

So, my friends, I encourage you to set clear and achievable goals for yourself. By doing so, you'll be taking an important step towards creating the life you truly want, and living your best life possible.

Embracing Discomfort And Taking Calculated Risks

As we embark on our journey to success, it is crucial to understand that growth and progress often come with discomfort and risk. It is easy to fall into the trap of comfort and complacency, but this mindset will not bring us the results we desire. Instead, we must learn to embrace discomfort and take calculated risks.

To achieve our goals, we must be willing to step outside of our comfort zones and face challenges head on. This may mean taking a new job, pursuing a new opportunity, or simply trying something new. While the unknown can be scary, it is also where the greatest growth and reward lies. By embracing discomfort, we open ourselves up to new experiences and new ways of thinking. This allows us to expand our horizons and reach new heights.

In addition to embracing discomfort, it is important to take calculated risks. This means being intentional about the risks we take and understanding the potential consequences. Before making a big decision, we should weigh the pros and cons and assess the likelihood of success. By doing so, we can make informed decisions that will help us reach our goals.

However, it is important to remember that taking risks does not mean blindly jumping into a situation without considering the consequences. Instead, we must approach each risk with caution and a clear understanding of the potential outcomes. This way, we can make decisions that are in our best interest and help us reach our goals.

Embracing discomfort and taking calculated risks are key to achieving our goals and reaching new levels of success. By stepping outside of our comfort zones, we open ourselves up to new experiences and opportunities. And by taking calculated risks, we can make informed decisions that will help us reach our goals. So let us embrace the unknown, take calculated risks, and never be afraid to pursue our dreams.

Building A Support System of People, Resources, And Tools

One of the key elements to bending your path is building a support system. Having a group of people, resources, and tools that can help you on your journey to manifestation can make all the difference.

Your support system can be composed of family, friends, colleagues, mentors, or a coach. These individuals should not only be supportive of your goals and dreams but should also hold you accountable to your plans and help you stay focused on your path. Having someone to share your struggles and triumphs with can help you maintain a positive and motivated attitude.

Additionally, resources such as books, audio recordings, workshops, and other learning materials can provide you with the information and insights you need to stay on track. In today's digital age, it is easier than ever to access resources that can support your growth and development. Take advantage of the vast knowledge base available to you, and keep yourself informed about the latest developments in your area of interest.

Finally, it's important to have tools that can help you stay organized and focused. This could include things like a daily planner, journal, or vision board. Whatever tools you choose, be sure they help you stay focused on your goals and keep you motivated.

Building a support system can help you overcome obstacles and keep you moving forward towards your goal. When you surround yourself with positive, supportive, and motivated individuals, it becomes much easier to achieve your desired outcomes. So take some time to build your support system and start seeing the results that come from having a strong support structure in place.

Embracing A Growth Mindset and Continuously Learning And Adapting

In life, the only constant is change. It is therefore essential that we embrace a growth mindset, one that recognizes that we can continuously learn, grow, and improve. With this mindset, we become proactive in seeking out new experiences and opportunities to develop and challenge ourselves. We also become more resilient, better able to overcome obstacles and challenges that arise.

One of the key components of a growth mindset is the belief that our abilities and intelligence are not fixed, but rather can be developed through effort and perseverance. This is in stark contrast to a fixed mindset, which holds that our abilities and intelligence are determined at birth and cannot be changed.

To embrace a growth mindset, it is essential that we cultivate a love of learning and a willingness to step outside of our comfort zones. This means taking calculated risks, trying new things, and being open to feedback and constructive criticism. We must also be willing to admit when we are wrong and make changes accordingly.

In order to achieve our goals and continuously grow, we must also have a strong support system in place. This includes people who believe in us, resources that can help us achieve our goals, and tools that will help us make progress.

One way to build a strong support system is to surround ourselves with people who share our values and goals. This can include friends, family members, mentors, or like-minded individuals. These people can provide us with encouragement, guidance, and support when we need it the most.

In addition to people, we must also have access to resources that will help us achieve our goals. This can include books, courses, workshops, or other forms of education that will help us develop new skills and knowledge. We must also be proactive in seeking out new resources as we need them, and be open to changing our approach when necessary.

Finally, we must have the right tools to help us achieve our goals. This may include a computer, a camera, a guitar, or other equipment that is necessary for us to pursue our passions. We must also be willing to invest in these tools, and to continuously upgrade them as we grow and evolve.

Embracing a growth mindset and continuously learning and adapting is essential to achieving our goals and fulfilling our potential. By surrounding ourselves with a strong support system of people, resources, and tools, and by being proactive in seeking out new experiences and opportunities, we can make our wildest dreams a reality.

CHAPTER 4
OVERCOMING
OBSTACLES

Obstacles can serve as doors to new opportunities, leading you to new paths you never considered before. Instead of seeing an obstacle as a dead end, view it as a chance to explore new possibilities and learn new things.

Take, for example, Thomas Edison. He failed over a thousand times in his quest to invent the light bulb, but he never gave up. He once said: "I have not failed. I've just found 10,000 ways that won't work."

Edison's persistence and refusal to give up in the face of obstacles ultimately led him to success and greatness.

Overcoming obstacles can help you build strength, character, and a sense of self-reliance. When you overcome challenges, you develop a greater sense of self-worth, self-esteem, and confidence. You also develop a deeper understanding of what you're capable of and what you can achieve. This can provide you with a sense of purpose and a sense of accomplishment.

The process of overcoming obstacles can be a growth-filled and empowering journey. With every obstacle you overcome, you become stronger, more resilient, and better equipped to handle future challenges. The journey to success is not always easy, but embracing obstacles and using them to your advantage can lead to personal growth, development, and the realization of your full potential.

Overcoming Obstacles: 7 Steps to Thrive

Obstacles in life are an inevitable part of our journey. It's not if we'll face challenges, but when. However, obstacles can be seen as opportunities to grow and become stronger. In this chapter, we'll explore seven ways to overcome obstacles and come out on top.

The way you think about obstacles plays a crucial role in your ability to overcome them. A positive mindset can make a big difference in how you perceive and handle challenges. Instead of seeing obstacles as insurmountable barriers, reframe them as opportunities to grow, learn, and become stronger. Having a clear and concise plan of action can make a big difference in overcoming obstacles. Start by setting realistic and specific goals that you want to achieve. This will give you a roadmap to follow and help you stay focused. It will also make it easier to track your progress and stay motivated.

Don't try to tackle obstacles on your own. Reach out to others for help and support. Surround yourself with positive and supportive people who believe in you and your ability to overcome obstacles. They can provide guidance, encouragement, and a fresh perspective when you need it most. Everyone makes mistakes, and that's okay. The key is to learn from them and use the lessons you've learned to grow and improve. Don't beat yourself up over setbacks. Instead, view them as opportunities to learn and grow.

Overcoming obstacles requires persistence and determination. Keep pushing forward, even when it seems like there's no end in sight. Remember why you started, and focus on your end goal. The more you persist, the more likely you are to overcome obstacles and achieve success. Fear of failure can hold us back and prevent us from overcoming obstacles. It's important to understand that failure is a natural part of the learning and growth process. Embrace failure and see it as an opportunity to learn and grow.

The world is constantly changing, and sometimes our plans may not work out. When this happens, it's important to stay flexible and adaptable. Be open to new ideas and opportunities that may arise. Be willing to pivot and make changes as needed to overcome obstacles and achieve your goals.

Overcoming obstacles takes time, effort, and a willingness to grow and improve. Embrace a positive mindset, set realistic and specific goals, seek help and support, learn from mistakes, stay persistent and determined, embrace failure, and stay flexible and adaptable. By following these steps, you'll be able to overcome obstacles and thrive in life.

Dealing With Fear And Self-Doubt

We all face obstacles in life, and one of the most significant obstacles we encounter is fear and self-doubt. These feelings can hold us back from pursuing our dreams and reaching our full potential. Fear and self-doubt can be powerful forces, but they can be overcome with the right tools and mindset. In this chapter, we will explore seven ways to deal with fear and self-doubt.

Identify and acknowledge your fear and self-doubt

The first step to overcoming fear and self-doubt is to identify and acknowledge it. This means recognizing the specific thoughts and feelings that are holding you back. Take some time to reflect on your thoughts and emotions, and write them down. This process can help you gain clarity and insight into the sources of your fear and self-doubt.

Challenge your negative thoughts and beliefs

Once you have identified your fear and self-doubt, it's time to challenge your negative thoughts and beliefs. Ask yourself if these thoughts are based in reality or if they are just limiting beliefs that are holding you back. Consider looking at the situation from a different perspective, and try to reframe your negative thoughts in a positive light.

Take action, even if it's uncomfortable

Taking action is one of the best ways to overcome fear and self-doubt. Start by taking small steps towards your goal, even if they are uncomfortable. This can help you build confidence and increase your resilience. As you gain more confidence, you can take on bigger challenges and continue to push yourself out of your comfort zone.

Surround yourself with positive and supportive people

The people you surround yourself with can have a significant impact on your thoughts and beliefs. Surrounding yourself with positive and supportive people can help you overcome fear and self-doubt by providing you with encouragement and motivation. Seek out mentors and people who have overcome similar challenges and can offer advice and guidance.

Focus on your strengths and accomplishments

It's important to focus on your strengths and accomplishments when dealing with fear and self-doubt. Keep a list of your accomplishments, and look at it when you are feeling discouraged. This can help you remember that you have the skills and abilities to overcome obstacles and reach your goals.

Practice self-compassion and self-care

It's important to be kind to yourself and practice self-compassion when dealing with fear and self-doubt. This means taking care of your physical, emotional, and mental well-being. Engage in activities that bring you joy, and make time for self-reflection and meditation.

Embrace change and uncertainty

Finally, it's important to embrace change and uncertainty when dealing with fear and self-doubt. Remember that life is a journey and that every encounter provides new potential directions. Be open to new opportunities and experiences, and trust in the journey, even if it leads you in unexpected directions.

Fear and self-doubt can be powerful obstacles, but they can be overcome with the right tools and mindset. By identifying and acknowledging your fear and self-doubt, challenging your negative thoughts and beliefs, taking action, surrounding yourself with positive and supportive people, focusing on your strengths and accomplishments, practicing self-compassion and self-care, and embracing change and uncertainty, you can overcome these obstacles and reach your full potential.

Overcoming with Emily

Once upon a time, there was a young woman named Emily who had always been interested in law. After graduating from law school with honors, she landed a job at a prestigious law firm in the city. Emily was eager to make a name for herself and was determined to succeed in the cutthroat world of corporate law.

However, she soon realized that her journey would not be easy. Her boss, a partner at the firm, was known for being tough and demanding. He seemed to enjoy putting his junior associates through grueling tasks and giving them impossible deadlines. Emily was no exception. She was given a high workload and expected to perform to the best of her abilities, even if that meant working long hours and sacrificing her personal life.

Despite the obstacles, Emily remained focused and driven. She took pride in her work and strived to excel in every task that was assigned to her. She was always willing to go the extra mile and do what was necessary to get the job done right.

However, her hard work and dedication did not go unnoticed by her boss. Over time, he began to take notice of her exceptional skills and started to rely on her more and more. Emily was soon promoted to a senior associate, and she continued to work hard and impress her superiors.

Years went by, and Emily's reputation as a skilled and diligent lawyer continued to grow. She was frequently asked to handle complex cases and was known for her ability to think outside the box and find creative solutions to difficult legal problems.

Finally, after years of hard work and perseverance, Emily was offered a partnership in the law firm. She was overjoyed and felt as though all of her efforts had paid off. She was now a full-fledged partner, and her future looked bright.

Emily continued to work tirelessly, building her reputation as one of the best lawyers in the city. She took on challenging cases and consistently exceeded her clients' expectations. Her colleagues respected and admired her, and she was soon known as one of the top lawyers in the country.

Years later, as she looked back on her journey, Emily was proud of all that she had accomplished. She had overcome countless obstacles and worked tirelessly to reach her goals. She was now a partner in one of the most prestigious law firms in the city, and her name was synonymous with success and excellence.

And she knew that no matter what obstacles lay ahead, she would always be ready to tackle them head-on and emerge victorious.

Overcoming The Hold of Fear

Fear affects everything in our lives. It permeates our thoughts, emotions, and actions, hindering us from reaching our full potential. The fear of not getting what we need or losing what we have is a common fear that many of us experience. This fear holds us back from experiencing joy and freedom in life.

However, it is important to recognize that everything in our lives comes from a place of love or fear. Most times, we are operating from a place of fear, limiting our growth and potential. But, when we can overcome the fear of dying, the rest of our fears tend to fade away. This is because, when we are no longer afraid of losing our lives, we are free to live life fully and authentically.

The source of our joy and happiness is within us, not outside of us. When we focus on things that don't matter, we distract ourselves from the beauty and potential that lies within. We are here to be the fullest expression of who we truly are, and this requires us to overcome the hold of fear in our lives.

There are two ways that fear manifests itself - the fear of not getting what we need and the fear of losing what we need. It's essential to understand that no one needs anything external to experience their true self. The things we think we need are just illusions, and when we can let go of these false beliefs, we will be able to see the world with a new perspective.

Fear affects everything in our lives, but it's up to us to overcome it. When we are no longer afraid of losing our lives, we are free to live life fully and authentically. The source of our joy and happiness is within us, and it's our job to tap into that inner wisdom and potential. Remember, we are here to be the fullest expression of who we truly are, and this requires us to overcome the hold of fear in our lives.

Bending Your Path: Properly Handling Setbacks And Failures

Setbacks and failures are a natural part of life, but how we handle them can have a significant impact on our overall success and happiness. Whether we're facing a major roadblock or just a minor setback, it's important to approach these challenges with a positive and proactive attitude. Here are some tips for properly handling setbacks and failures:

1. Acknowledge and Accept the Reality: The first step in overcoming setbacks and failures is to acknowledge and accept the reality of the situation. This means acknowledging that the setback has happened and accepting that it's part of the journey.

2. Take Responsibility: It's easy to blame others or external factors for our setbacks, but taking responsibility for our own actions and decisions is key to overcoming them. This doesn't mean accepting blame or fault, but rather acknowledging what we could have done differently and learning from the experience.

3. Learn From the Experience: Every setback and failure provides an opportunity for growth and learning. Take the time to reflect on what you can learn from the experience, and use that knowledge to help you grow and move forward.

4. Seek Support: No one can succeed alone, and seeking support from friends, family, or a support group can help you overcome setbacks and failures. Having someone to talk to and share your experiences with can help you gain new perspectives and stay motivated.

5. Stay Positive: It's important to maintain a positive attitude and outlook, even when facing setbacks and failures. This can be

challenging, but reminding yourself of your strengths and accomplishments, focusing on the good in life, and practicing gratitude can help you stay positive and motivated.

6. Develop a Plan: Once you have processed the setback or failure, it's time to develop a plan for moving forward. This may mean developing a new strategy, making adjustments to your approach, or simply taking a step back and regrouping.

7. Keep Moving Forward: The final step in overcoming setbacks and failures is to keep moving forward. This means taking action, staying focused on your goals, and maintaining a positive and proactive attitude, even when things get tough.

Remember, setbacks and failures are a natural part of life, but how we handle them can make all the difference in our success and happiness. By acknowledging and accepting the reality of the situation, taking responsibility, learning from the experience, seeking support, staying positive, developing a plan, and keeping moving forward, you can bend your path and overcome any obstacle in your way.

Path Benders Keep Motivation And Momentum Going

In life, it's easy to get sidetracked, lose focus and lose motivation. This can lead to setbacks, delays, and even failure. However, those who bend their path and keep motivation and momentum going, will have a greater chance of success. Here are a few ways to stay motivated and keep your momentum going:

1. Set Specific and Measurable Goals - Having clear and specific goals that are measurable will give you a sense of purpose and direction. This will help you stay motivated and focused on what you need to do in order to reach your desired outcome.

2. Keep Your Vision In Mind - Your vision is a powerful motivator, it's what keeps you going even when times get tough. Keeping your vision in mind will help you overcome setbacks and failures.

3. Celebrate Small Wins - Celebrating small wins along the way will give you a sense of accomplishment and help keep your motivation and momentum going. Recognize and celebrate your progress, no matter how small it may seem.

4. Stay Positive - Staying positive, even in the face of challenges and obstacles, is critical to keeping your motivation and momentum going. Positive thinking will give you the energy and drive you need to keep pushing forward.

5. Surround Yourself with Positive People - The people you surround yourself with can have a big impact on your motivation

and momentum. Surround yourself with people who support and encourage you, and who will lift you up when you're feeling down.

6. Keep Learning and Growing - Personal and professional growth is important for keeping motivation and momentum going. Make a commitment to continue learning and growing, and be open to new ideas and opportunities.

7. Reward Yourself - When you reach a major milestone or achieve a significant goal, reward yourself. This can be a simple treat like a special meal, a relaxing spa day, or a trip. Whatever it is, make sure it's something that you'll enjoy and that will keep you motivated and focused on your goals.

By keeping motivation and momentum going, Path Bending can be challenging, but it's not impossible. By setting specific and measurable goals, keeping your vision in mind, celebrating small wins, staying positive, surrounding yourself with positive people, keeping learning and growing, and rewarding yourself, you can bend your path and achieve great success.

Path Benders Build Resilience And A Positive Attitude

Once upon a time, there was a woman named Sarah who was determined to make a change in her life. She was tired of feeling stuck and defeated every time she faced challenges and setbacks. Sarah wanted to be someone who could handle anything that life threw her way with grace and positivity.

So, she decided to become a Path Bender. She knew that this would require her to have a resilient spirit and a positive attitude, no matter what obstacles she faced. She was determined to make this a reality and so, she set out on her journey.

Sarah's first obstacle came in the form of a job loss. She had worked at the same company for years and had just been let go due to budget cuts. Sarah was devastated and felt like all of her hard work had gone to waste. But instead of wallowing in her sadness, she took a deep breath and reminded herself that she was a Path Bender.

She knew that this setback was just a temporary obstacle and that she would bounce back from it. So, she dusted herself off and got to work. She updated her resume, reached out to her network and started applying for new jobs. Sarah also used this time to reflect on what she really wanted in her career and what steps she needed to take to get there.

A few weeks later, Sarah landed a job that was even better than the one she had lost. It was in her dream field and offered her a better salary and more opportunities for growth. Sarah was thrilled, but she also knew that her journey as a Path Bender was far from over.

Throughout the rest of her career, Sarah faced many challenges and setbacks. But each time, she used her resilience and positive attitude to overcome them. She never let her setbacks define her and instead, used them as opportunities to grow and become a better version of herself.

Years went by and Sarah's hard work and determination paid off. She was promoted to a leadership position in her company and was recognized as a role model for her colleagues. People admired her for her resilience and positive attitude, and often sought her out for advice and support.

Sarah was proud of the person she had become and knew that her journey as a Path Bender had been worth every step. She was grateful for the challenges and setbacks she faced along the way, because they helped her build the resilience and positive attitude that she needed to succeed in life.

In the end, Sarah's story serves as a reminder that no matter what obstacles we face, we have the power to bend our path and become the person we truly want to be. All it takes is a little resilience, a positive attitude, and the determination to never give up.

CHAPTER 5: RETURN AND SURRENDER

SURRENDER

Understanding the Goal

Once upon a time, there was a woman named Jane. She had been through many struggles and hardships in her life, and often felt like she was just going through the motions. However, one day, she stumbled upon the idea of the Infinite Intelligence, and it completely changed her perspective.

Jane learned that the Infinite Intelligence was the source of all knowledge and power, and that it was within her reach if she just opened herself up to it. She became fascinated by this concept and spent hours researching and learning about it. As she delved deeper, she realized that her goal in life should be to align herself with the Infinite Intelligence and allow it to guide her path.

Jane began to understand that the goal was to find the path of least resistance in everything she did. This meant letting go of resistance, allowing things to flow naturally, and embracing the journey instead of focusing solely on the destination.

One of the key things Jane learned was that love was a powerful force that could be harnessed to tap into the Infinite Intelligence. She discovered that love did not have just one frequency, but could be experienced in many different ways. This realization allowed her to see that she did not need anyone else to access her full potential and tap into the Infinite Intelligence.

With this newfound understanding, Jane began to shift her focus from external sources of happiness to the source of joy within her. She stopped wasting her time and energy on things that didn't matter, and instead began to concentrate on being the fullest expression of who she truly was.

As she continued on this path, Jane found that she was becoming more and more resilient. Her positive attitude and unwavering motivation kept her momentum going, and she was able to handle setbacks and failures with ease.

In the end, Jane became a shining example of how understanding the goal can lead to a life of joy, fulfillment, and success. She was a true "Path

Bender", who had learned how to bend her path towards the Infinite Intelligence and reach her full potential.

Harnessing the Power of Emotion

The Law of Attraction is a powerful force in the universe, but it is often misunderstood. People think that they need to focus their thoughts and mental energy on what they want in order to attract it into their lives. While this is important, it is not the only factor at play. Your emotions play an equally important role in manifesting your desires.

Think of your emotions as the fuel that powers the Law of Attraction. If you care deeply about something and feel a positive, passionate emotion about it, then the Law of Attraction will respond to that energy and bring it into your life. On the other hand, if you have resistance or negative emotions about a certain outcome, the Law of Attraction will not respond in the same way.

So, how do you harness the power of your emotions to attract what you want? The key is to identify what you truly care about, and then to focus on those emotions to the exclusion of everything else. When you are in touch with your emotions and feel a deep connection to your desires, the Law of Attraction will respond and bring them into your life.

It is also important to let go of any resistance or negative emotions that may be holding you back. This means letting go of fear, doubt, and any other limiting beliefs that are blocking your path. When you are able to let go of these obstacles, you will be able to tap into the power of your emotions and the Law of Attraction will work in your favor.

So, remember, your emotions are a key factor in attracting what you want in life. Focus on what you care about, let go of any resistance, and tap into the power of your emotions to bring your desires into reality. With time and practice, you will see just how powerful the Law of Attraction can be when you harness the power of your emotions.

HOW TO SURRENDER AND WIN

In a small village in feudal Japan, there lived a samurai warrior named Kenji. He was known for his incredible strength, skill with a sword, and fearless attitude. Kenji was proud of his reputation as one of the strongest warriors in the land and was always eager to prove his worth in battle.

One day, Kenji was tasked with a mission to defeat a powerful enemy who was threatening the peace of the village. Despite the odds being against him, Kenji was confident in his abilities and set off on his mission with a fierce determination.

However, things quickly took a turn for the worse. Kenji's opponent was more powerful and skilled than he had anticipated, and he was soon defeated in battle. The samurai warrior was badly wounded and left for dead on the battlefield.

Kenji's defeat was a wake-up call for him. He realized that his pride and arrogance had blinded him to the reality of the situation, and that he could not rely solely on his strength and skills to win. He needed to learn the ways of surrender and understand the true meaning of victory.

Over the next few months, Kenji recuperated from his injuries and began to study the art of surrender. He practiced meditation and mindfulness, and learned to let go of his ego and focus on the present moment. He also spent time training with a wise old master who taught him the ways of the Path Bender.

The old master taught Kenji that surrender was not about giving up, but about letting go of the things that held him back. He explained that Path Benders were able to navigate the challenges of life with grace and ease because they understood that the universe was always working in their favor.

Finally, the day came when Kenji was ready to put his newfound understanding of surrender to the test. He was given another chance to face his enemy in battle, and this time, he approached the fight with a new mindset. Instead of trying to force his way to victory, Kenji surrendered to the moment and let the universe guide him.

To everyone's surprise, Kenji emerged victorious from the battle. He had finally learned the true meaning of surrender and victory, and had become a Path Bender. He now lived his life with a newfound sense of purpose and peace, using the lessons he had learned to navigate the challenges of life with ease and grace.

From that day forward, Kenji was known as the Path Bender Samurai, and his story was told for generations to come. People came from far and wide to hear his teachings and learn from his wisdom. Kenji had suffered greatly before he became a Path Bender, but in the end, it was all worth it.

Tapping Into Infinite Expansion

In the world we live in, there is an endless stream of potential, growth, and progress available to us all at every moment. This is the Infinite Expansion, an ever-present energy source that surrounds us and holds endless possibilities for us to tap into. The key to unlocking this vast pool of potential is to understand and harness the power of our own energy and vibration. This is what allows us to tap into the Infinite Expansion and experience a state of flow, where everything comes to us with ease and grace.

Athletes are well aware of this phenomenon, often referring to it as "the zone." They understand that when they are in the zone, their thoughts and actions are in complete alignment with their goals, allowing them to perform at their highest level. They tap into the Infinite Expansion by being completely present in the moment, letting go of all resistance and fear, and trusting in their own abilities. This state of flow allows them to move effortlessly through their sport and achieve their goals with ease.

So, how do you tap into the Infinite Expansion? The first step is to get into receiving mode. This means that you must be open and receptive to the energy that surrounds you, allowing it to flow through you freely. It is about letting go of limiting beliefs, releasing resistance, and trusting that the universe has your back. When you align yourself with the energy of the Infinite Expansion, you will find that opportunities and solutions will come to you more easily and that you will have a greater sense of purpose and direction in your life.

Another important aspect of tapping into the Infinite Expansion is to focus on your emotions. Your emotions are the guiding force that let the

Law of Attraction know which thoughts and experiences to bring into your life. When you focus on positive emotions, such as love, joy, and gratitude, you raise your vibration and attract more of those experiences into your life. Conversely, when you focus on negative emotions, such as fear, anger, and frustration, you lower your vibration and attract more of those experiences into your life.

Tapping into the Infinite Expansion is a powerful tool for living a life of abundance, happiness, and purpose. By aligning yourself with the energy that surrounds you, focusing on positive emotions, and getting into receiving mode, you can tap into this infinite source of potential and experience a life filled with limitless opportunities. Remember, the world is an ever-expanding universe, and you have the power to expand with it.

Aligning with Your True Path

As you continue on your journey of understanding the Infinite Intelligence and becoming a Path Bender, your next goal should be to strive for alignment in every aspect of your life. Alignment means being in harmony with your true self and the path that you are meant to follow.

It is important to understand that when you are in alignment, everything that you desire will come to you with ease. The Universe, through the Law of Attraction, will bring you what you want because there is no resistance blocking the flow of abundance. This is because when you are in alignment, you vibrate at a high frequency and the Universe responds by providing you with more of what you want.

However, many people often cloud their connection to the Infinite Intelligence by putting things in their body and mind that are not in alignment with their true path. This can include unhealthy habits, negative thoughts, and limiting beliefs. All of these things can cause pain and discomfort, as they disconnect you from your true path and the power of the Infinite Intelligence.

The Intelligence Running your body is always in a place of good vibration and non-resistance, so it is essential to be mindful of the things that you are putting into your body and mind. By doing this, you will be able to tap into the infinite expansion and receive all of the abundance that the Universe has to offer.

Alignment in every area of your life should be your second goal on your journey to becoming a Path Bender. When you are in alignment, everything that you desire will come to you with ease, and you will experience the joy and fulfillment that come from living in harmony with your true self. Remember, you are here to live a life of joy, love, and abundance, so strive to be in alignment with your true path and the Infinite Intelligence at all times.

The Unserving Beliefs

As humans, we all have a set of beliefs that shape our perception of the world and how we interact with it. Unfortunately, many of these beliefs can actually work against us, leading to unfulfilled desires and a sense of dissatisfaction with life.

The first step to overcoming this problem is to understand that your beliefs are not set in stone. They are not absolute truths, but rather a collection of thoughts and experiences that you have accumulated over time. Some of these beliefs are based on your own experiences, while others may have been imposed on you by others, such as family, friends, and society.

One of the most common ways that unserving beliefs can manifest is through unfulfilled desires. If you have desires that remain unfulfilled, it is likely that you hold beliefs that are not aligned with those desires. This can happen because the beliefs you have adopted may be in alignment with someone else's opinions, rather than your own.

For example, some people believe that committed relationships are solely about property, rather than love and intimacy. This belief can prevent them from experiencing the love and connection that they desire in a relationship.

Another example is the belief that sex and committed adulthood are not related. This can lead to feelings of frustration and dissatisfaction, as well as unfulfilled desires.

It is important to recognize that these beliefs are not facts, but rather opinions that have been shaped by your experiences and the people in your life. By identifying and challenging these unserving beliefs, you can start to shift your perspective and align with your true desires.

The key to overcoming unserving beliefs is to examine your thoughts and beliefs, and determine which ones are truly serving you and which ones are not. This process can be difficult, as it may require you to challenge long-held beliefs and beliefs that are deeply ingrained in your thought patterns.

However, by taking the time to question and understand your beliefs, you can start to create new, more empowering beliefs that align with your desires. This will allow you to live a life that is more in alignment with your true nature and help you to achieve the things that you truly want.

It is important to recognize that your beliefs have a profound impact on your life. By identifying and challenging unserving beliefs, you can create a more fulfilling and satisfying life, filled with the love, connection, and abundance that you truly desire.

The Path of Least Resistance

As a Path Bender, you must understand the importance of embracing the path of least resistance in your journey towards alignment and fulfillment. The common misconception is that suffering and struggle are necessary in order to reach your goals and desires. However, this is not the case.

The truth is that suffering only occurs when you are not in alignment with your true self and the infinite intelligence that surrounds you. It is a sign that you are on the wrong path, that you are not in a state of least resistance.

The key to avoiding suffering and reaching your alignment is to understand that you do not need to endure hardship in order to reach your goals. Instead, you must focus on getting into a state of least resistance and allowing the infinite intelligence to guide you to your desires.

When you are in a state of least resistance, you are in perfect alignment with the infinite intelligence and with your true self. This means that you are vibrating at a high frequency and that you are open to receiving all the abundance and fulfillment that the universe has to offer.

So, the third goal of a Path Bender is to know that you are not supposed to get to your alignment only after suffering. Instead, you must learn to get into least resistance and perfect alignment without ever having to suffer. By embracing this goal, you will be able to experience a life of abundance and fulfillment, free from the pain and struggle that so many people endure.

Remember, the path of least resistance is the path that leads to your true alignment and your greatest desires. So, embrace this path and trust the infinite intelligence to guide you towards a life of abundance and joy.

Sergeant Mike Thomas

Sergeant Mike Thomas had seen and experienced more pain and suffering in his time serving in the Vietnam War than most people could ever imagine. The war had taken its toll on his body and his mind, but he had never lost the hope that he would make it out alive.

Mike was a hard-headed soldier who never backed down from a fight, but as the days went by and the casualties piled up, he began to realize that the path of fighting and resistance was not the way to survive. He was constantly surrounded by death and destruction, and he knew that he had to find a new way to navigate through the chaos if he wanted to make it out alive.

One day, while on a reconnaissance mission, Mike was separated from his unit and found himself lost in the jungle. He was alone, surrounded by enemy forces, and he was running low on supplies. As he sat there, pondering his next move, he remembered the lessons he had learned from his training back home. He remembered his third goal - to know that he was not supposed to get to his alignment only have he suffered majorly.

Mike closed his eyes and took a deep breath, focusing on his inner self. He tried to feel the power of the Infinite Intelligence running through his body, and he felt a surge of energy flow through him. He opened his eyes and saw a path before him, a path of least resistance. He knew that this was the way to survive.

He began to walk down this path, letting his emotions guide him and surrendering to the flow of the universe. He walked for what felt like hours, and eventually he stumbled upon a small village that was occupied by friendly forces. He was safe and had made it out alive.

From that moment on, Mike had a newfound respect for the power of surrender and the path of least resistance. He had learned that suffering was not necessary to reach his ultimate goal of survival. Instead, he had discovered a new way of being - a way of tapping into the Infinite Intelligence and letting it guide him to safety.

Mike went on to become a respected leader in the military, and he shared his lessons with his fellow soldiers. He was a shining example of how to bend the path and find the way to least resistance, even in the face of war and destruction.

RETURN TO SOURCE

You ARE the Creator

As the soldier journeyed through the war, he had come to a realization. He was not just a bystander in his life, a victim to the circumstances and events that surrounded him. He had a power within him that he never knew existed, a power that would shape and mold his reality. The soldier realized that he was the creator of his own reality.

This understanding was a turning point in the soldier's journey. He saw that his thoughts, beliefs, and emotions were the driving force behind the experiences he was having in his life. The events and circumstances that he had once seen as uncontrollable and out of his hands were actually being shaped by him. He was the one responsible for the pain and suffering he had been through.

The soldier knew that this understanding would take some time to master, but he was determined to put it into practice. He started paying close attention to his thoughts, beliefs, and emotions. He saw that when he was in alignment with what he truly desired, he was in a state of peace and joy. But when he was in resistance, he was in a state of fear and anxiety.

The soldier realized that the key to his reality was to get into a state of least resistance, to be in alignment with his desires. He learned to tap into the infinite intelligence and let it guide him to his path of least resistance. He found peace in the chaos of war, knowing that he was the one in control of his reality.

With this newfound understanding, the soldier was able to survive the war and return home as a changed man. He had transformed from a victim to a creator, from a sufferer to a path bender. The soldier was now in control of his reality and lived a life filled with joy, peace, and abundance. He knew that he was the creator of his own reality and nothing could stand in his way.

Understanding The Law of Attraction

As a creator of your own reality, it is crucial to understand the law of attraction and how it works in your life. The law of attraction states that what you focus on, you bring into your reality. This means that the things you think about, the things you talk about, and the things you believe, are all reflected in your life.

Many people are not aware of the power of their thoughts and beliefs. They often go through life reacting to the things that happen to them instead of creating the life they want. They spend their time focusing on the problems instead of finding solutions and finding the blessings in their life.

This is why it is important to understand that you are the creator of your own reality. You are in charge of what comes back to you, and you can choose to create a reality that is filled with positivity and blessings. When you focus on the things you want, you are attracting them into your life.

However, when you spend most of your time thinking about the things you don't want, you are attracting those things into your reality as well. This is why it is important to give yourself a break and allow all the negative momentum you have built up to fade away. This may take some time, but it is crucial to your success in creating the life you want.

It is also important to understand that when you see something as a problem, the source within you is always seeing those things as a solution. This is why you may feel bad when you are going against the real you. To align with your true self, it is important to shift your focus to solutions and find the blessings in every situation.

The law of attraction is a powerful tool in creating the life you want. By focusing on the things you want and finding solutions to the challenges you face, you are creating a reality that is filled with positivity, blessings, and abundance. Remember, you are the creator of your own reality, and you have the power to shape your life in the way you desire.

Source Energy

Jesus is known throughout history as a healer, a man who could cure people of their diseases and ailments simply by laying his hands on them. But what many people do not understand is the secret behind his healing powers: Source energy.

Source energy refers to the pure and infinite life force that flows through all things, including every living being. This energy is the source of all creation, and it is what powers the universe and everything in it.

Jesus was so connected to Source energy that he was able to tap into it and use it to heal those who were suffering. He never saw the illness in a person, but instead saw their wellness, their innate state of health and wholeness. This allowed him to channel the healing power of Source energy into the person, helping them to regain their health and vitality.

This is a lesson for us all. We too can tap into Source energy and use it to bring about healing and change in our own lives. By connecting with this infinite and powerful energy, we can become more in tune with our own inner wisdom and intuition, and better understand our own paths towards wellness and fulfillment.

So, the next time you find yourself feeling stuck or uncertain, try taking a moment to connect with Source energy. Close your eyes, breathe deeply, and allow yourself to feel the flow of this infinite life force within you. As you tap into this energy, you will begin to feel more connected to the universe, and more capable of bringing about positive change in your life.

The Power of Source

Once upon a time, there was a business man named David who had built his company from the ground up. He had a loving wife and a young son, but as his business started to struggle, he began to feel the weight of the world on his shoulders. Despite putting in long hours and working tirelessly, he couldn't seem to get back on track.

As the stress of his business mounted, David's relationship with his wife began to suffer. Tired of the constant struggling, she eventually left him and took their son with her. With his family gone and his business failing, David found himself homeless and alone.

One day, as he sat on the streets corner with his few possessions, he looked at his son and something stirred in him. In that moment, he remembered that he was not just a struggling business man, but also a part of Source Energy.

Determined to turn his life around, David began to focus on his connection to Source Energy. He meditated and visualized success, imagining himself and his business thriving. Slowly but surely, things started to change.

Opportunities began to present themselves, and with a newfound sense of confidence, David was able to secure a loan to get his business back on track. He worked tirelessly, pouring all of his energy into making the business a success.

As his business started to grow, David's wife and son noticed the changes in him and were drawn back to his side. They were amazed by the transformation they saw in him and were grateful to be a part of his life once again.

In the end, David realized that his struggles had been a gift in disguise. Through his journey to reconnect with Source Energy, he had learned to tap into his inner strength and resilience. He was now a stronger, more confident man, and his business was thriving as a result.

David was proof that no matter how tough the journey may be, with the right mindset and a connection to Source Energy, anyone could achieve their wildest dreams.

Tapping Into Infinite Expansion

The journey to becoming the master of your own reality, to tap into the Infinite Expansion and to Surrender to the understanding of being Source Energy, can be a long and difficult one. But with each step taken, with each obstacle overcome, you are brought closer to the ultimate realization of your true potential.

It may take time and patience, but the reward is immeasurable. A life filled with abundance, joy, and love. A life where you have the power to shape your own reality and create the experiences you desire.

When you align yourself with the energy of the universe and allow yourself to be guided by the wisdom of your innermost being, anything becomes possible. Every moment is an opportunity for growth and transformation. Every moment is a chance to tap into the infinite expansion and allow your desires to flow effortlessly into your life.

So, embrace the journey and trust in the wisdom of your innermost being. Remember that you are Source, and that with every breath, you are expanding into the infinite. With every step, you are becoming more and more connected to the truth of who you truly are. And when you fully surrender to this understanding, every desire you have will enter your experience with ease, and you will be able to live the life of your dreams. The power to shape your reality and to create the life you desire is within you. Embrace it, surrender to it, and watch as the universe conspires to bring your dreams to life.

I encourage you to embrace the truth about who you are: a being of infinite power, wisdom, and potential. When you surrender to this understanding, you tap into a limitless source of energy and creativity, unlocking the full potential of your life. You are not limited by your past experiences, your fears, or the beliefs of others. You are not a victim of circumstance, but the master of your own reality. When you realize this, you unleash the power within you to shape your life in any way you choose.

So, as you close this book, we invite you to make a powerful choice. Choose to surrender to your true identity as a being of Source energy. Choose to tap into the infinite expansion of the universe, and to align yourself with the flow of abundance and joy that is always available to you. When you make this choice, you will discover that anything is possible. You will find the courage to overcome any challenge, the wisdom to navigate any situation, and the power to manifest your deepest desires.

So, be bold. Be daring. And be confident in the knowledge that you are Source. Period. When you live from this understanding, every experience you have, every person you meet, and every moment of your life will be infused with new meaning and purpose. So, take this moment to close your eyes, take a deep breath, and surrender to the infinite power within you. And know that from this moment forward, you are on a path of infinite expansion, abundance, and joy.

Congratulations on your journey, and may you continue to thrive and flourish as a being of Source energy.

PART TWO THE MISCONCEPTION OF STRUGGLING

BECOME A PATH BENDER TODAY

https://assemblyofwanderers.com/path-bender

CHAPTER 6: WE HAVE IT ALL WRONG

The human experience is full of ups and downs, and it's natural to feel like we're struggling at times. But what if we told you that struggling is just a misconception? What if we told you that you can live a life without struggle, without constantly battling against the odds, and without feeling like you're constantly falling short? It's true. Struggling is just a thought pattern that we've adopted, a way of perceiving the world that keeps us stuck in a cycle of hardship and discomfort.

It's easy to fall into the trap of believing that struggle is just a part of life, that it's inevitable and that we just have to endure it. But this couldn't be further from the truth. Struggle is not a fact of life, it's a choice. And the reason we struggle is because we've bought into the idea that we have to work hard, fight against the odds, and constantly push ourselves to the limit in order to achieve our goals and find success.

But what if we told you that success and abundance can be effortlessly achieved simply by tapping into the infinite expansion that's happening all around us? That by returning to our true essence as Source, we can live a life of ease and flow, where every desire we have enters into our experience and every obstacle surrenders before us?

In part two, we're going to explore the misconception of struggling and show you how to tap into the infinite expansion to create a life of abundance and fulfillment. By the end of this book, you'll understand the true nature of reality, the power of your thoughts and beliefs, and how to align with the infinite expansion to effortlessly manifest your desires. So get ready to let go of the struggle and embrace the infinite expansion of abundance and success.

Poverty Is Not Holy

For centuries, poverty has been portrayed as a holy and noble state, something to be revered and respected. This notion has been deeply ingrained into many cultures and religions, leading to the belief that struggling and suffering are necessary steps to reach spiritual enlightenment. This concept, however, couldn't be further from the truth. Poverty is not holy, and it is not something to be glorified.

The misconception of poverty as a holy state is deeply ingrained in many cultures and religions. It is often believed that one must give up material wealth and live a life of deprivation to become closer to a higher power. This idea is rooted in the belief that material wealth is a hindrance to spiritual growth, and that true enlightenment can only be achieved by living a life of poverty.

However, this belief is not only untrue but it can also lead to negative consequences. By accepting poverty as a holy state, people may become resigned to their struggles, feeling that they are unworthy of abundance and prosperity. This mindset can keep individuals trapped in a cycle of poverty and struggling, leading to a life filled with stress, anxiety, and suffering.

It is essential to understand that poverty is not holy, and it is not something to be revered. The Universe is abundant and provides ample opportunities for growth and prosperity, regardless of one's financial status. The idea that poverty is necessary for spiritual growth is simply a limiting belief, and one that must be challenged.

Breaking away from traditional and religious teachings can be difficult, but it is a necessary step to achieve true prosperity and abundance. To do this, it is essential to question your beliefs, examine your values, and align your thoughts and actions with a new, more empowering perspective. It is time to break away from the misconception of poverty as a holy state and embrace the idea that prosperity and abundance are our birthright.

It is time to reject the notion that struggling and suffering are necessary for spiritual growth. Instead, embrace the truth that the Universe is abundant and provides ample opportunities for growth and prosperity. When you align your thoughts, beliefs, and actions with this truth, you will find that abundance and prosperity come easily and effortlessly into your life. So, embrace the idea that you are worthy of abundance and prosperity, and take the necessary steps to claim it as your own.

The Common Misconceptions of Emotions and Manifestations

The world has been taught that emotions and manifestations are something to be feared, suppressed, and ignored. However, this is a common misconception that has led many individuals down a path of self-doubt and unfulfillment. Emotions and manifestations are not things to be feared, but rather powerful tools that can be harnessed to create the life you desire.

One of the biggest misconceptions about emotions is that they are something to be suppressed. Many people believe that emotions are negative and therefore should be avoided or ignored. However, emotions are not negative or positive, they simply are. Emotions are an important part of who we are and they provide valuable information about what is happening within us. When we suppress our emotions, we are not only avoiding our true selves, but we are also missing out on the powerful guidance they provide.

Another common misconception about emotions is that they are things that happen to us. This is not true. Emotions are not things that happen to us, but rather things that are created by us. Every emotion we experience is a result of our thoughts and beliefs. This means that we have the power to choose our emotions and to create the emotional state that serves us best.

Manifestations are another area where misconceptions abound. Many people believe that manifestations are only for the lucky few who have some kind of special talent. However, this could not be further from the truth. Manifestations are not only for the lucky few, but they are a natural part of the human experience. Every thought and emotion we have is a manifestation, whether we realize it or not. When we understand this, we can use our thoughts and emotions to consciously create the life we desire.

It is important to dispel the common misconceptions about emotions and manifestations. Emotions are not negative or positive, they are simply a part of who we are. Manifestations are not just for the lucky few, but a natural part of the human experience. When we understand this, we can use our emotions and manifestations to create the life we desire. By embracing our emotions and harnessing the power of our thoughts, we can create a life filled with joy, abundance, and fulfillment.

The Misconception of Death as the Path to Heaven

Throughout history, many people have held the belief that death is the only way to reach heaven, the ultimate paradise where they will live in everlasting peace and happiness. This idea has been ingrained in cultures and religions worldwide and has been passed down from generation to generation. However, this notion is nothing but a misunderstanding of the true nature of reality and the role of our emotions in creating our experiences.

The idea that death is the only way to reach heaven has led people to view life as a struggle, full of hardships and suffering, with only the promise of heaven after death to comfort them. This way of thinking has contributed to a mentality of resignation and hopelessness, where people have given up on creating a life of abundance and joy for themselves and their loved ones. The belief that life is a struggle and that heaven is only accessible through death has become a self-fulfilling prophecy, as people continue to experience hardship and suffering because they believe that is what life is all about.

However, this is far from the truth. In reality, you are not limited to the experiences that you have created for yourself, and you have the power to create a life of abundance, joy, and prosperity while you are still alive. You are the Creator of your own reality, and your emotions and thoughts are the tools that you use to manifest your experiences. If you focus on feelings of love, gratitude, and abundance, you will create a life that reflects these emotions, and you will experience heaven on earth.

It is time to break away from the traditional and religious teachings that have taught us that poverty is holy, and that death is the only way to reach heaven. Instead, embrace the truth that you are Source Energy, and that you have the power to create a life of abundance and joy while you are still alive. The Universe is abundant, and there is enough prosperity, love, and joy to go around for everyone. It is time to claim your share of this abundance and live the life you were meant to live, filled with joy and happiness.

Embrace the truth that you are the Creator of your own reality and that you have the power to manifest a life of abundance and joy. The journey to heaven is not a journey that you take after death, but a journey that you take while you are still alive, filled with prosperity, love, and joy. So, go ahead and create the life you want, and live in heaven on earth.

Through The Eyes of John

Once upon a time, there was a preacher named John. John was a man of faith who had dedicated his life to spreading the word of God and helping his church members lead a better life. He was a kind and compassionate man who truly cared for the people in his community.

However, as time went by, John began to notice a disturbing trend in his congregation. Despite their best efforts, many of the people in his church were struggling financially. They were living from paycheck to paycheck, struggling to make ends meet, and often going without the things they needed.

John felt a deep sense of frustration and sadness at this situation. He had always taught his church members about the importance of living a virtuous and holy life, but it seemed that no matter how hard they tried, they were still struggling.

One day, as John was praying for guidance, he had an epiphany. He realized that he had been focusing too much on the idea that poverty was holy, and not enough on the idea of abundance and prosperity. He realized that God wanted his children to live a good life and to enjoy the blessings that life had to offer.

With this newfound understanding, John set out to change the way he taught. He started talking to his congregation about the importance of wise financial management and investing their money. He encouraged them to take control of their financial situation, and to work towards a brighter future.

At first, many of the people in his congregation were skeptical. They had been taught for so long that poverty was a virtue, and that it was necessary to sacrifice their wants and needs in order to achieve spiritual enlightenment. But John persisted, and slowly but surely, people started to change their minds.

John's teachings had a profound impact on the lives of the people in his congregation. They began to take control of their finances and to invest in their future. They learned how to enjoy life, while still being good stewards of their resources.

In the end, John's message of abundance and prosperity was a huge success. The people in his congregation were able to improve their financial situation, and to live a life filled with joy and abundance. They realized that they could be both holy and prosperous at the same time, and they were grateful to John for teaching them this important lesson.

And so, John's story serves as a reminder to us all that God wants us to live a good life, filled with abundance and prosperity. By breaking free from the misconception that poverty is holy, and embracing the idea of abundance and prosperity, we can achieve a brighter future for ourselves and for those around us.

The Importance of Experiencing and Analyzing Desires

Desires are a crucial part of our lives, they drive us to achieve great things, push us out of our comfort zones and inspire us to grow. However, many of us often fall into the trap of wanting something simply because society or our peers have deemed it as desirable, without truly understanding why it is that we desire it. This leads to unfulfilled desires and a sense of dissatisfaction with our lives.

To truly make the most of our desires and harness their power, it is important to take the time to experience and analyze them. This means being mindful of what it is that we truly desire, and why we desire it. Is it something that we truly want for ourselves, or is it something that has been imposed upon us by others?

Once we have a clear understanding of our desires, we can start to work towards fulfilling them in a way that aligns with our values and purpose. This can involve setting clear goals and taking practical steps to achieve them, but it can also involve letting go of desires that no longer serve us and embracing new ones that are more in line with who we are and what we want to achieve.

It is also important to understand that our desires can change over time as we grow and evolve, and that this is a natural part of the journey. By being open to change and embracing our desires, we can experience a sense of fulfillment and joy in our lives that is not dependent on external circumstances.

In short, experiencing and analyzing our desires is a crucial step towards living a fulfilling and purposeful life. By taking the time to understand what it is that we truly desire and why, we can unlock the power of our desires and use them to create the life that we truly want.

CHAPTER 7: UNDERSTANDING THE PURPOSE OF ANALYZING DESIRES

Desires are an integral part of the human experience. They drive us, motivate us, and give us direction. But not all desires are equal. Some are aligned with our true nature, while others may not serve us. This is why it is important to analyze our desires, to understand what they truly represent and what they can teach us.

The purpose of analyzing desires is to gain insight into the beliefs and patterns that are driving us. Our desires are a reflection of what we believe to be possible, what we believe we deserve, and what we believe is important. When we analyze our desires, we can begin to see the underlying beliefs that are shaping our reality.

Analyzing our desires can also help us to identify areas in our lives where we may be struggling or where we need to make changes. For example, if we find that we constantly desire material possessions, it may indicate that we have an underlying belief in lack or scarcity. By examining this desire, we can work to shift this limiting belief and create a more abundant reality.

It is also important to understand that our desires are not just about what we want in the present moment. They are also a reflection of our deepest desires and aspirations, the things that we truly long for in our lives. When we analyze our desires, we can begin to uncover our true purpose and find the path that will lead us to greater fulfillment and happiness.

Analyzing our desires is a powerful tool for personal growth and transformation. It helps us to understand the underlying beliefs and patterns that shape our reality and provides us with valuable insights into our true nature and purpose. So, take the time to reflect on your desires and what they are telling you about yourself. This journey of self-discovery will bring you closer to realizing your full potential and experiencing the abundance and joy that is your birthright.

The Consequences of Not Analyzing Desires

Desires play a significant role in our lives, serving as the driving force behind our choices and actions. However, if we don't take the time to analyze our desires, we could be setting ourselves up for disappointment and even failure. The consequences of not analyzing desires are numerous and can have a significant impact on our lives.

One of the main consequences of not analyzing desires is unfulfilled expectations. When we don't take the time to think about our desires and what we really want, we may make impulsive decisions or go after things that seem appealing at the moment but aren't really aligned with our true goals and values. This can lead to disappointment and frustration when we don't get what we thought we wanted.

Another consequence of not analyzing desires is lack of motivation. When we don't have a clear understanding of what we want and why, it can be difficult to stay motivated and focused on our goals. Without a clear direction, it's easy to become discouraged and lose sight of what we're working towards.

In addition to these internal consequences, not analyzing desires can also have external consequences. For example, if we're not clear about what we want, we may end up making decisions that are not in our best interest. This could mean accepting a job offer that doesn't align with our values, or investing in a business that doesn't have the potential for success.

Furthermore, not analyzing desires can also lead to financial difficulties. If we're not careful about what we're spending money on, we may end up overspending or making investments that aren't wise. This can result in debt, financial stress, and other financial challenges that can impact our quality of life.

Analyzing desires is an important step in creating the life we want. By taking the time to think about what we really want, why we want it, and how it fits into our overall goals and values, we can avoid the consequences of not analyzing desires and set ourselves up for success.

A Prisoner of False Desires

Once upon a time, there was a man named John who lived a comfortable life. He had a good job, a loving family, and enough money to support them all. Despite all this, John was never truly happy. He felt like something was missing and he couldn't quite put his finger on what it was.

John had desires, of course, but he never took the time to analyze them. He simply went through life, chasing after things that he thought would make him happy. He bought material possessions, took expensive vacations, and even started drinking more to numb his feelings of dissatisfaction.

However, all these things only brought temporary happiness and the emptiness still lingered. John never took the time to understand what his true desires were and what was truly important to him. He was so caught up in trying to fill the void, that he never stopped to think about why he was feeling empty in the first place.

One day, John's life took a turn for the worse. He lost his job, his wife left him, and his money began to run out. He was left with nothing but his alcohol addiction and a feeling of utter despair. He realized that the life he had built for himself was built on false desires and empty promises. He had never truly understood what he wanted out of life, and now he was paying the price for it.

John hit rock bottom and was forced to confront the consequences of not analyzing his desires. He realized that if he wanted to turn his life around, he had to start from the beginning and understand what was truly important to him. He sought help for his alcohol addiction and started to look within himself to find the answers he had been searching for all along.

Slowly, John began to see the world in a new light. He discovered what his true desires were and started to take steps to fulfill them. He realized that the key to happiness was not in the material possessions or temporary fixes, but in understanding himself and his desires.

John's life changed for the better and he finally found the happiness he had been searching for. He was grateful for the hard lessons he learned and was determined to never make the same mistake again. He started to teach others about the importance of analyzing their desires and finding true happiness within themselves.

In the end, John was no longer a prisoner of his own false desires. He was free to live a life full of purpose and fulfillment. He was proof that it is never too late to change your life and find happiness, as long as you are willing to understand and analyze your desires.

OVERCOMING IS AN UNBALANCED ACTION

Obstacles can be seen as an opportunity to grow and challenge ourselves, but often, we focus solely on overcoming them instead of finding a balance between the obstacle and our desired outcome. This approach can lead to a sense of desperation and a single-minded pursuit of success, causing us to forget about the other important aspects of our lives.

When we focus solely on overcoming an obstacle, we create an unbalanced action, which can cause us to become overly consumed by the task at hand. This can lead to burnout, stress, and an unhealthy relationship with our desired outcome. In extreme cases, it can also cause us to ignore our own health and well-being, leading to negative consequences in the long run.

Additionally, by focusing solely on overcoming obstacles, we often miss out on the other opportunities and experiences that life has to offer. This unbalanced approach to success can leave us feeling unfulfilled and lacking a sense of purpose.

In order to find balance, it is important to remember that success is not just about overcoming obstacles, but also about enjoying the journey. By taking the time to reflect on our desires, values, and priorities, we can create a holistic approach to success that is both fulfilling and sustainable.

By finding this balance, we can overcome obstacles in a way that enhances our overall well-being and enriches our lives. By focusing on both the end goal and the journey, we can create a sense of purpose and fulfillment, allowing us to achieve our goals while also enjoying the process.

The Impermanence of Overcoming

The law of energy conservation states that energy cannot be created or destroyed, only transformed from one form to another. This fundamental principle of physics serves as a reminder that everything in the universe is connected and constantly changing.

It can be tempting to try and overcome obstacles in our lives, but this approach often leads to an unbalanced action. We push against what we perceive as negative and resist what is. The more we resist, the more entrenched the obstacle becomes.

The key is to understand that obstacles are not permanent, they are merely a temporary manifestation of energy in flux. The obstacle is not the problem, it is the perception of the problem that creates the suffering. The solution lies in becoming at peace with the obstacle, not in trying to overcome it. When we surrender to the natural flow of energy, we can transform the obstacle into an opportunity for growth and learning.

Embracing the impermanence of life and the natural flow of energy is a powerful way to break free from the constraints of our limiting beliefs. It is a path to inner peace, and a way to align with the infinite wisdom of the universe.

So, instead of trying to overcome obstacles, let us become at peace with them. Let us embrace the natural flow of energy, and transform our experiences into opportunities for growth and learning. By doing so, we align with the infinite wisdom of the universe, and open ourselves to limitless possibilities.

Embracing Life's Experiences

In life, we all have experiences, some good and some bad. It's essential to understand that these experiences shape us and make us who we are. However, it's not just about having experiences, but also about understanding, accepting and sharing them. Understanding our experiences can give us a deeper insight into our lives, allowing us to reflect and grow from them.

Accepting our experiences, whether positive or negative, is a crucial step in personal growth. When we resist or deny our experiences, we block ourselves from learning and moving forward. By accepting our experiences, we can release any negative emotions or thoughts that may be hindering our progress.

Sharing our experiences with others can also be incredibly healing. It gives us a sense of community and support, and allows us to connect with others who have gone through similar situations. Sharing our experiences can also provide a source of inspiration and encouragement for others, as well as allowing us to gain a fresh perspective on our own experiences.

It's important to remember that everyone's experiences are unique and valuable, and that we can learn and grow from each other's stories. By embracing life's experiences, we can create a rich tapestry of life, filled with growth, understanding, and connection.

Understanding, accepting, and sharing our experiences is a powerful tool for personal growth and connection. So let's embrace life's experiences and use them to create a richer and more meaningful life.

What Happens When You Don't Embrace Life's Experiences

Once upon a time, there was a woman named Mary who was married to a man named Tom. Mary was a person who lived in her own world and never wanted to experience anything new. She was always afraid of change and was not willing to try anything new. She always lived in the comfort zone and never wanted to step out of it.

Tom, on the other hand, was an adventurous person and always wanted to experience new things. He tried to convince Mary to try new things and step out of her comfort zone, but she never wanted to listen. Tom would go out and explore new places, meet new people, try new foods, and do new activities, but Mary would always say no.

One day, Tom decided to plan a surprise trip for Mary, hoping that she would finally embrace new experiences. He took her to a beautiful island where they could go scuba diving, explore the local culture, and try new foods. However, Mary was not happy about this trip. She was scared and uncomfortable, and she never wanted to leave the resort. Tom tried his best to make her happy and comfortable, but she was still unhappy.

Eventually, Tom realized that Mary's lack of willingness to embrace new experiences was affecting their relationship and their happiness. He tried to talk to her and convince her to try new things, but she was not willing to listen. Tom realized that he needed to let Mary be and live her life the way she wanted, even if it meant not having her by his side.

After Tom left, Mary realized how much she missed the adventures and experiences that she could have had with Tom. She realized that life was not just about living in her comfort zone, but about embracing new experiences and learning from them. She realized that she had missed out on so much and decided to embrace new experiences and embrace life to the fullest.

In the end, Mary became a completely different person. She was open to new experiences, and she was happy and full of life. She learned the importance of embracing new experiences and how it can change her life for the better. She finally understood why Tom always wanted her to embrace new experiences and she was grateful for his patience and understanding.

CHAPTER 8: THE JOURNEY TO ASCENSION THROUGH EXPERIENCE

In life, it's common to want to take shortcuts and avoid obstacles. We believe that if we can just overcome the challenges we face, we'll finally reach the place of peace and prosperity that we desire. But what if we told you that this way of thinking is not only misguided, it's also preventing you from truly ascending to the next level?

You see, the Universe is not about avoiding obstacles or taking shortcuts. Instead, it's about experiencing them, learning from them, and growing from them. When you go through your trials and tribulations, you become a better, stronger, and more resilient person. You become someone who is better equipped to handle whatever life throws your way, and who can truly thrive in the face of adversity.

So instead of trying to overcome your obstacles, embrace them. Allow yourself to fully experience them, without resistance or judgement. And as you go through each experience, pay attention to the lessons that are being revealed to you. The Universe is always speaking to you, even through the most difficult of experiences.

And as you begin to understand the importance of embracing life's experiences, you'll start to see that the journey to ascension is not a quick fix or a shortcut, but a lifetime of growth, expansion, and learning. So let go of the need to overcome anything, and instead become at peace with every experience that comes your way. In doing so, you'll find yourself ascending to new heights, both personally and spiritually.

It's Always The Proper Time for Every Person

Have you ever found yourself in a difficult situation and wondered why it was happening to you? Have you felt frustrated or hopeless because things seemed to be going wrong no matter what you did? It's important to remember that everything happens in the proper time for every person. There is no such thing as a mistake or a setback, only opportunities for growth and evolution.

The universe is always guiding us towards our highest good, and every experience we have, whether positive or negative, serves a purpose.

Sometimes we need to go through trials and tribulations in order to learn important lessons and become stronger and wiser. We may not always understand why something is happening in the moment, but looking back we can often see how it was necessary for our growth and evolution.

It's easy to get caught up in the idea that we need to overcome obstacles and avoid negative experiences, but this can actually be a short cut to ascension. The universe wants us to go through all of our trials and tribulations so that we can be a better person and ascend to a higher level of consciousness. When we resist or try to avoid these experiences, we prevent ourselves from learning the lessons we need to learn and growing in the way we are meant to.

By accepting that there are no mistakes and that everything happens in the proper time for every person, we can approach life with a sense of peace and understanding. We can trust that the universe is always guiding us towards our highest good and that every experience, no matter how difficult, is serving a purpose.

Next time you find yourself in a difficult situation, try to see it as an opportunity for growth and evolution. Trust that the universe is always guiding you towards your highest good, and that everything happens in the proper time for every person. By embracing this perspective, you can approach life with a sense of peace and understanding, knowing that everything is happening exactly as it should.

There Are No Mistakes

Max was a young, ambitious man who had always dreamed of making it big in the business world. He had worked hard all his life to save up enough money to start his own company and finally, the day had come. He was ready to take the leap and invest all of his savings into his new venture.

However, he made the biggest mistake of his life. He invested in a startup that promised to be the next big thing, but it turned out to be a scam. Max lost all of his money and was left with nothing. He was devastated and felt like his life was over.

Days turned into weeks and weeks into months, and Max found himself struggling to make ends meet. He took on any job he could find, but it seemed like no matter what he did, he just couldn't get back on his feet.

One day, as he was walking down the street, Max saw a casting call for a new TV show that was looking for entrepreneurs to compete for a chance to win a large sum of money. Max had always been a fan of these shows, and he thought it could be a good opportunity to get his life back on track.

He applied and was surprised when he was selected as one of the contestants. The show was a huge hit and Max quickly became a fan favorite. He was known for his creativity, tenacity, and charisma, and before he knew it, he was the last one standing and had won the grand prize.

But the real prize was yet to come. The show had made Max a household name, and he was suddenly inundated with offers from investors who wanted to work with him. He used the money he won on the show to start a new company, and this time, he made sure to do his due diligence and research before investing.

Max's new company was a huge success and made him a millionaire many times over. He had finally achieved his dream and was living the life he had always wanted. But he never forgot the mistake he made that led him to where he was today. He used it as a lesson and always made sure to be careful and cautious with his investments.

Max learned that sometimes, the biggest mistakes can lead to the biggest opportunities. He was grateful for the opportunity that had come his way and never took his success for granted. He continued to work hard, stay humble, and never lost sight of the journey that had brought him to where he was today.

ACCEPTING THAT EVERYTHING IS PERFECT

A Journey to a Better Reality

Max had always been a hard worker and strived for success. He believed that success was the key to happiness and that was what he was determined to achieve. But, after losing all his savings, Max felt like he had hit rock bottom. He was miserable and angry, blaming everyone and everything for his misfortune. He was filled with bitterness towards the world and the people in it.

One day, as he was walking through the park, Max bumped into an old friend who he hadn't seen in years. They started talking and Max vented to his friend about his frustrations with life. The friend listened patiently and then said something that would change Max's life forever.

"Max, you have to understand that everyone is creating their perfect reality. They are doing the best they can with what they have. You can't control their actions, but you can control your own. You can create your own reality, too."

Max was taken aback by his friend's words. He had never thought about it like that before. He realized that he had been so focused on blaming others for his problems that he had lost sight of his own power. He could create his own reality and he didn't have to accept the actions of others.

Max decided to take control of his life and start creating his own reality. He started to meditate and focus on his thoughts and feelings. He realized that he was the only one who could make himself happy and that he didn't need anyone else's approval to do so.

Max began to see the world in a different light. He started to appreciate the people in his life and the experiences he was having. He realized that everyone was doing the best they could and he could learn from them and their experiences.

With this newfound perspective, Max's life changed dramatically. He started a new business and it took off. He was finally in control of his life and he was creating the reality he wanted. He was happy and successful, and he owed it all to accepting the actions of others and creating his own reality.

Max was now a millionaire and he was grateful for the lesson he learned. He never forgot that everyone is creating their perfect reality and that he could create his own, too. He lived a happy and fulfilling life and he was an inspiration to everyone around him.

Max's story showed that accepting the actions of others should never be a hard thing because everyone is creating their perfect reality. By accepting that, he was able to create his own reality and live a life that he was proud of.

The Victim and Oppressor in Reality Creation

Max had always been fascinated by the concept of reality creation. He had studied philosophy and spirituality, always searching for answers to how the mind could shape one's surroundings. But he never considered the role of power dynamics in this process until he met a wise woman named Sarah.

Sarah explained to Max that in any given situation, there were always two opposing forces at play: the victim and the oppressor. These roles were not limited to individuals in positions of power and control; they could exist in any relationship or situation. The victim was someone who felt oppressed, powerless, and at the mercy of external circumstances. The oppressor was the one who held power over the victim and made decisions that impacted their lives.

Max was shocked to realize that he had often played both the role of victim and oppressor in his own life. He had felt oppressed by his financial situation and had taken out his frustrations on others, including his loved ones. But he also remembered times when he had been the victim, feeling helpless and powerless in the face of life's challenges.

Sarah helped Max to understand that the victim and oppressor dynamic was not set in stone. In any given moment, one could choose to shift their perspective and take back control of their reality. By accepting responsibility for their thoughts and emotions, one could move from the victim role to the role of the creator.

Max was skeptical at first, but Sarah's words resonated with him, and he decided to put them into practice. He started by becoming more aware of his thoughts and emotions and how they were affecting his reality. He learned to reframe his negative thoughts and take control of his emotional responses. He practiced letting go of the need to control others and began to see himself as the creator of his own reality.

As he continued to practice, Max began to see incredible changes in his life. He was no longer a victim of his financial situation but instead saw himself as the creator of his financial reality. He let go of the need to control others and instead focused on creating a supportive and loving environment for himself and those around him.

Max's transformation was not without challenges, but with each new insight and shift in perspective, he felt more and more empowered. He realized that accepting the actions of others was not a hard thing because everyone was creating their perfect reality. And with this realization, he embraced his role as a creator and began to live the life of his dreams.

Max's journey showed him that the dynamic between the victim and oppressor was not permanent and that anyone could take back control of their reality by accepting responsibility for their thoughts and emotions. By choosing to see himself as the creator of his reality, Max had found the key to living a life filled with joy, abundance, and purpose.

CHAPTER 9: KARMA

The Origins of Karma - Understanding Our Ancestral Beliefs

The concept of karma has been an integral part of Eastern philosophy for thousands of years. The earliest references to the idea can be traced back to ancient Hindu and Buddhist scriptures, where it was believed that the laws of cause and effect governed all of existence.

In Hinduism, the concept of karma was linked to the idea of reincarnation. It was believed that the actions and deeds of a person in this life would determine their fate in the next. If a person acted in a virtuous manner, they would reap the rewards in the form of a favorable rebirth. On the other hand, if they acted immorally, they would suffer the consequences in their next life.

In Buddhism, the idea of karma was seen as a natural law that governed the cycle of birth, death, and rebirth. It was believed that every thought, word, and deed had a corresponding effect, and that the consequences of these actions would inevitably come back to the individual in the form of good or bad karma.

In both Hinduism and Buddhism, the ultimate goal was to attain liberation from the cycle of reincarnation and achieve a state of enlightenment. By living a virtuous life, individuals could accumulate positive karma that would help them move closer to this goal.

Our ancestors believed that karma was a way to promote justice and fairness in the world. They saw it as a way to ensure that people were held accountable for their actions, and that the consequences of their actions would be felt in this life or in a future life.

They also believed that karma was a way to encourage individuals to live virtuous lives. By understanding that their actions had real consequences, people were motivated to act in ways that would bring about positive outcomes.

The idea of karma has its roots in ancient Hindu and Buddhist philosophies, where it was seen as a natural law that governed the cycle of birth, death, and rebirth. It was believed that every thought, word, and deed had a corresponding effect, and that the consequences of these actions would inevitably come back to the individual in the form of good or bad karma. Our ancestors saw karma as a way to promote justice and fairness, and to encourage individuals to live virtuous lives.

The Adoption of Karma into Christianity

As Christianity began to spread throughout the world, it encountered various cultures and beliefs, including the concept of karma. The early Christian missionaries, who sought to convert as many people as possible, were faced with a challenge. How could they convince people with deeply ingrained beliefs in karma to embrace the Christian faith? To overcome this challenge, the missionaries adapted and integrated the idea of karma into their teachings.

One of the first examples of this integration was seen in the writings of St. Augustine, a prominent early Christian theologian. In his works, Augustine acknowledged the idea of good deeds leading to good consequences and bad deeds leading to bad consequences, much like the concept of karma. He argued that this concept was consistent with the principles of Christianity, as the idea of reward and punishment for one's actions was already established in the Bible.

Over time, the idea of karma became a central part of Christian teachings, especially in the form of the concept of divine justice. This idea held that God, as the ultimate judge, would reward good deeds and punish bad deeds in the afterlife. This mirrored the idea of karmic retribution, as both concepts held that one's actions would determine their ultimate fate.

The adoption of the idea of karma into Christianity was not without controversy, however. Some theologians argued that it was incompatible with the teachings of Christianity, as the Bible emphasized God's grace and mercy rather than strict retribution. Nevertheless, the idea of karma became so firmly ingrained in Christian teachings that it remains a central part of the faith to this day.

This integration of karma into Christianity not only made the faith more appealing to converts, but it also allowed the early Christians to better understand and explain the complexities of the world around them. By incorporating the idea of karma into their beliefs, they were able to provide a coherent explanation for why some people experienced good fortune while others suffered. This helped to allay fears and provide comfort to those who struggled to make sense of the world.

The integration of the idea of karma into Christianity was a gradual process that took place over several centuries. However, by adopting this belief, early Christians were able to expand their understanding of the world and provide comfort to those in need. Today, the idea of karma remains a central part of the Christian faith, and it continues to shape the way many people view the world and their place in it.

Karma In The Urantia Book

The book *The Urantia Book* explores the concept of karma in great detail, offering a unique perspective on the subject. According to this book, karma is the result of choices made by individuals and is a natural law of the universe. It explains that the universe operates on the principles of cause and effect, and that every action has a corresponding effect.

The book also states that karma is not a system of punishment or reward, but a means of helping individuals grow and evolve. It explains that every experience, whether positive or negative, is an opportunity for growth and learning. The book states that individuals can use their experiences to become better, more enlightened beings.

One of the key themes of the book is that individuals are responsible for their own lives and experiences. It explains that we create our own reality through our thoughts, words, and actions, and that we are the architects of our own destiny. The book also states that individuals have the power to change their lives and experiences by changing their thoughts, words, and actions.

In *The Urantia Book*, the concept of reincarnation is also linked to karma. It explains that individuals have multiple lifetimes to learn, grow, and evolve, and that they carry the consequences of their actions from one lifetime to the next. The book states that reincarnation provides a means of balancing the effects of our actions, allowing individuals to learn from their experiences and grow.

In conclusion, the book *The Urantia Book* offers a unique and detailed perspective on the subject of karma. It explains that karma is a natural law of the universe and a means of helping individuals grow and evolve. By embracing the principles of cause and effect, individuals can use their experiences to become better, more enlightened beings.

Karma In The Law of One

In *The Law of One, The Ra Contact*, karma is explained as a fundamental law of the universe, governing the interactions and experiences of all beings. According to the book, every thought, word, and deed has an impact on the universe and creates a ripple effect, influencing future events and experiences.

Karma is described as a means of balancing the energies of the universe. Every action generates a certain amount of energy, either positive or negative, and this energy must be balanced in some way. If a person engages in actions that generate positive energy, they will experience positive consequences, while actions that generate negative energy will result in negative consequences.

The book explains that the concept of karma is tied to the idea of reincarnation. The energies generated by our actions follow us from one life to the next, creating the conditions for our next incarnation. This means that the experiences we have in this life are influenced by our past actions, and the actions we take in this life will influence our future experiences.

The idea of karma is closely tied to the concept of free will. The book explains that, while our experiences are influenced by our past actions, we always have the power to choose our own path and make our own decisions. We are not bound by the consequences of our past actions, but we are influenced by them.

The book stresses that the ultimate purpose of karma is not punishment or reward, but growth and evolution. The experiences we have in each lifetime are opportunities to learn, grow, and evolve as beings. By understanding and embracing the law of karma, we can use our experiences to become better and more enlightened beings.

The Law of One, The Ra Contact provides a comprehensive explanation of the concept of karma, showing how it influences our experiences and provides opportunities for growth and evolution. The book emphasizes the importance of making conscious choices and understanding the impact of our actions on the universe, as well as on ourselves.

The Law of One, The Ra Contact, presents a unique view on karma as a tool for personal and spiritual growth. The book explains that karma is not just a mechanism for balancing the universe, but a means of advancing the soul. Our experiences, both positive and negative, are opportunities for growth and development. Through these experiences, we can learn about our own nature and the nature of the universe, and use that knowledge to advance to higher levels of consciousness.

The book explains that each soul has a unique path of growth and evolution, and that the experiences we have in each lifetime are part of that path. The law of karma operates on the principle of cause and effect. Our thoughts, words, and actions have consequences, and these consequences shape our experiences in future lifetimes. If we act in negative or harmful ways, we will experience negative consequences in the future. If we act in positive and beneficial ways, we will experience positive consequences.

Karma is simply a means of creating opportunities for growth and evolution. The experiences we have are designed to teach us about our own nature and the nature of the universe. By embracing the law of karma and using our experiences to learn and grow, we can evolve into more enlightened beings.

The book also explains that karma operates at both the individual and collective levels. Our actions not only shape our own experiences, but they also have an impact on the collective consciousness. The collective consciousness is shaped by the thoughts, words, and actions of all beings, and it in turn shapes our individual experiences. By understanding the law of karma and working to create positive experiences, we can help to raise the collective consciousness and create a better world for all beings.

The book also explains that our understanding of the law of karma is directly tied to our level of spiritual awareness. As we become more aware of the consequences of our actions, we can make choices that are more in alignment with our path of growth and evolution. By doing so, we create a positive and beneficial reality for ourselves and those around us.

For the rest of this chapter, we will focus on a holistic view of karma as a tool for personal and spiritual growth. By embracing the law of karma and using our experiences to learn and grow, we can advance on our path of evolution and become better, more enlightened beings.

A Story of Karma and Evolution

Once upon a time, there was a young man named David who lived in a small village. He lived a simple life and was well-liked by everyone in the village. Despite his popularity, David felt like he was missing something in life. He felt as though there was more to the world than what he was experiencing and he yearned for something greater.

One day, a strange man named Marcus came to the village. Marcus was wealthy, charming, and seemed to have all the answers to David's questions about the world. David was drawn to Marcus and soon became his protégé. Under Marcus's guidance, David learned about the law of karma and how it affected everyone's lives.

David was fascinated by the idea that everything we do and experience is simply a means of growth and evolution. He was determined to use his experiences to become a better and more enlightened person. However, Marcus had a different understanding of karma. He saw it as a means to manipulate others and gain power over them.

As David's mentor, Marcus taught him many things, but he also instilled in him a sense of greed and entitlement. Marcus was a master manipulator and David became his willing accomplice. The two of them worked together to exploit the villagers and amass wealth and power.

Despite their success, David began to feel a sense of guilt and unease about what he was doing. He began to see the negative effects of their actions on the village and its people. David tried to talk to Marcus about his concerns, but Marcus dismissed them, saying that the law of karma was on their side.

David was torn between his loyalty to Marcus and his growing sense of morality. Eventually, his conscience won out and he decided to turn against Marcus and make amends for the harm they had caused. He used his newfound understanding of the law of karma to help the villagers and heal the wounds that he and Marcus had inflicted.

In the end, David realized that karma is not a tool for punishment or reward, but a means of growth and evolution. By embracing the law of karma and using his experiences to learn and grow, he became a better and more enlightened person. He lived the rest of his life as a wise and respected elder in the village, serving as an example of how embracing the law of karma can lead to personal growth and a more fulfilling life.

The Purpose of Karma: Growth and Evolution

Karma is a concept that has been around for thousands of years and is central to many spiritual and philosophical belief systems. The word karma is derived from the Sanskrit word "kri," which means "to do." The law of karma states that every action we take, every thought we have, and every word we speak creates a chain reaction that determines the course of our lives. Simply put, the law of karma is a principle of cause and effect.

The purpose of karma is not to punish or reward us, but to provide us with opportunities for growth and evolution. Our experiences in each lifetime are designed to teach us about ourselves and the universe. Every experience is a lesson, and every lesson is a step along the path of our spiritual journey.

Karma is not a one-time event, but a continuous process. Our thoughts, words, and actions create patterns in our lives that shape our experiences. Over time, these patterns form the fabric of our reality, and they determine the direction of our lives. We are always creating our own karma, and everything that happens to us is a reflection of the choices we have made.

The idea that everything comes back to karma is rooted in the idea of the circle of life. The law of karma states that every action we take has consequences, and those consequences shape our experiences in future lifetimes. This creates a continuous cycle of cause and effect that determines the course of our lives.

The cycle of karma is not limited to this lifetime. It is a journey that continues from one lifetime to the next. Our experiences in each lifetime are opportunities to learn, grow, and evolve, and the law of karma provides us with the tools we need to do so. By embracing the law of karma, we can use our experiences to become better and more enlightened beings.

In conclusion, the purpose of karma is to provide us with opportunities for growth and evolution. Everything that happens to us is a reflection of the choices we have made, and the law of karma is simply a means of guiding us along the path of our spiritual journey. By understanding and embracing the law of karma, we can use our experiences to become better and more enlightened beings, and create a better reality for ourselves and others.

Forgiveness Stops The Wheel of Karma

The concept of karma is closely tied to the idea of cause and effect. Our actions in this life and previous lives create ripples of consequences that shape our future experiences. However, the idea of forgiveness provides a powerful tool for breaking the cycle of karma.

When we forgive someone, we release the resentment, anger, and bitterness that can hold us back from growth and evolution. Holding onto negative emotions creates a negative energy within us that attracts similar experiences and perpetuates the cycle of karma. By forgiving, we are able to let go of this negative energy and create space for new and positive experiences.

Forgiveness is not about excusing harmful behavior or forgetting what has happened. It is about releasing our attachment to the past and freeing ourselves from the cycle of karma. When we forgive, we are taking responsibility for our own happiness and wellbeing. We are choosing to break the cycle and create a new reality for ourselves.

In the end, forgiveness is a powerful tool for spiritual growth and evolution. By embracing the power of forgiveness, we can transform our lives and create a brighter future for ourselves and those around us. Whether we are seeking to heal from past hurts or simply seeking to grow as individuals, forgiveness is an essential step in the journey.

The Law of One, the Ra Contact, explains that forgiveness is a critical component of understanding and working with the law of karma. The book emphasizes that forgiveness is not just about letting go of past wrongs and hurts, but about recognizing the interconnectedness of all beings and the fact that we are all playing our own unique role in the journey of growth and evolution.

According to *The Law of One*, all beings are connected and we are all part of a greater consciousness. When we act in negative or harmful ways, we not only harm others, but we also harm ourselves, as our actions create ripples that affect the entire consciousness. Conversely, when we act in positive and loving ways, we contribute to the growth and evolution of the entire consciousness.

The Law of One teaches that forgiveness is a critical component of breaking the cycle of negative karma. When we forgive, we release the negative energy that has been generated by our past actions, and this energy is transformed into positive energy that contributes to our growth and evolution.

Forgiveness also helps us to understand the nature of our experiences and the experiences of others. By recognizing that our experiences are a result of the choices we have made, and that others' experiences are a result of their own choices, we can see that all beings are playing their own unique role in the journey of growth and evolution.

In essence, The Law of One teaches that forgiveness is not just about letting go of past wrongs, but about recognizing the interconnectedness of all beings and using our experiences to evolve into more enlightened beings. By embracing the principle of forgiveness, we can break the cycle of negative karma and contribute to the growth and evolution of the entire consciousness.

CHAPTER 10: SEEING THE WORLD LIKE A PATH BENDER

The Law of One and Newton's First Law of Motion

The Law of One and Newton's First Law of Motion are two seemingly disparate ideas that are actually deeply connected. The Law of One, as presented in the Ra Contact, is a spiritual and philosophical teaching that explains the nature of reality and our place in the universe. Newton's First Law of Motion, on the other hand, is a scientific law that governs the behavior of physical objects. Yet, despite their differences, these two ideas can be seen as two sides of the same coin.

The Law of One teaches that everything in the universe is interconnected and that every thought, word, and action we take has a ripple effect that impacts the world around us. This is similar to Newton's First Law of Motion, which states that an object at rest will remain at rest unless acted upon by an unbalanced force. In other words, everything in the universe is in a state of balance unless acted upon by an external force.

Both the Law of One and Newton's First Law of Motion emphasize the idea of balance. The Law of One teaches that we must strive to maintain balance in our thoughts, words, and actions in order to create positive outcomes. This is similar to Newton's First Law of Motion, which states that everything in the universe seeks to maintain balance unless acted upon by an external force.

In both the Law of One and Newton's First Law of Motion, the concept of force is central. In the Law of One, the force is our thoughts, words, and actions. In Newton's First Law of Motion, the force is any external force acting upon an object. However, both teachings emphasize the idea that force creates change and that the outcome of that change is determined by the balance or imbalance of the force.

The Law of One and Newton's First Law of Motion both emphasize the importance of balance and the impact that our thoughts, words, and actions have on the world around us. While these two ideas may seem disparate, they are actually deeply connected and both contribute to our understanding of the world and our place in it.

The Power of Oneness: The Benefits of Seeing the World as One Interconnected Piece

In a world that often encourages division and separation, being a path bender requires a different perspective. Path Benders understand that everything and everyone is interconnected, and that separation is just an illusion. They see the world as one big, interconnected piece, and they reap many benefits from this perspective.

One of the biggest benefits of this worldview is that it helps to eliminate judgment and division. When you see everything as interconnected, it becomes much harder to judge others or to view the world in terms of "us versus them." Path Benders understand that everyone is just doing the best they can, and that every person is an integral part of the larger whole.

Another benefit of seeing the world as one interconnected piece is that it allows for a more holistic view of the world. Path Benders understand that everything is connected, and that the health and wellbeing of one aspect of the world affects everything else. For example, they might see the destruction of the rainforest not just as a loss of a unique ecosystem, but as a loss for the entire planet.

In addition, seeing the world as one interconnected piece allows Path Benders to cultivate a sense of interdependence and community. They understand that they are part of a larger community, and that they have a role to play in the health and wellbeing of that community. This sense of interdependence encourages Path Benders to take actions that benefit not just themselves, but the entire community as well.

Ultimately, being a path bender requires a shift in perspective, away from division and separation, and towards interconnectedness and oneness. By embracing this worldview, Path Benders can reap many benefits, including a reduction in judgment, a more holistic view of the world, and a sense of interdependence and community.

The concept of a Path Bender is a powerful one, as it highlights the idea that we have the ability to shape and mold our own lives, rather than being subject to the whims of fate or circumstance. The idea that we can bend our own path, rather than simply following the path that is set before us, is an empowering one, and has the potential to drastically change the way that we think about ourselves and the world around us.

One of the key benefits of seeing the world as one interconnected piece is that it allows us to view every experience and situation as an opportunity for growth and development. When we understand that everything is connected, we are able to see each experience as part of a larger pattern, and we can begin to understand the purpose and meaning behind each event. This shift in perspective can help us to approach each experience with a sense of curiosity and wonder, rather than fear or negativity.

Another key benefit of seeing the world as one interconnected piece is that it allows us to see the illusion of separation for what it truly is. When we understand that everything is connected, we can see that all beings and experiences are essentially the same, and that our sense of separation is simply an illusion that we have created for ourselves. This understanding can help us to break down the walls of division and hatred, and to see each person and experience as a reflection of ourselves.

Finally, seeing the world as one interconnected piece can have a profound impact on our personal growth and spiritual journey. When we understand that everything is connected, we can begin to understand the nature of our own being and the purpose behind our existence. This understanding can help us to evolve and grow as individuals, and to experience a deeper sense of connection and meaning in our lives.

The idea of a Path Bender is a powerful one, and has the potential to greatly impact our lives. By seeing the world as one interconnected piece, we can begin to see every experience and situation as an opportunity for growth and development, and we can begin to understand the illusion of separation for what it truly is. With this understanding, we can evolve and grow as individuals, and experience a deeper sense of connection and meaning in our lives.

The Beginning of The Last Path Bender

It had been years since the prophecy of the last Path Bender was made. The world had moved on, and people no longer believed in the idea of bending their paths. It was considered a legend, a myth passed down from ancient times. However, there was still a small group of people who held onto the belief, and they were the ones who had been keeping an eye out for the last Path Bender.

Our protagonist, whose name was Max, was a young man who had always felt like he was destined for something great. He had always been an outsider, never quite fitting in with the rest of the world. But he had always felt a deep connection to the idea of Path Bending, and he had always known that he was different from everyone else.

When the prophecy of the last Path Bender was made, Max's life changed forever. Suddenly, he was no longer an outsider. He was the subject of interest for many, and many came to him, asking for his help in finding the ancient secret that was said to be hidden within the mechanized cave.

Max was at first doubtful of the prophecy. He didn't think he was the last Path Bender, and he didn't believe that he would be able to uncover the ancient secret. But as time passed, he began to feel a sense of purpose, a sense of destiny that he couldn't ignore.

One day, while exploring the hills near his home, Max stumbled upon a hidden entrance to a mechanized cave. It was a place no one had ever been, and it was said to hold the ancient secret that the Path Benders had been searching for. Max didn't think twice before entering the cave.

As he made his way deeper into the cave, Max could feel the energy around him change. He could sense that he was getting close to the ancient secret. And then, in the deepest part of the cave, Max found it. It was a large, glowing crystal that was emitting a bright light. Max felt drawn to the crystal, and as he approached it, he could hear a voice speaking to him.

"You are the last Path Bender," the voice said. "You have been chosen to unlock the power of the crystal. Only you have the strength and the courage to do so."

Max was scared, but he knew that he had to unlock the crystal. He stepped forward and reached out to touch it, and as soon as he did, he was enveloped in a bright light. When the light faded, Max felt different. He felt stronger, and he felt like he had a new understanding of the world.

The ancient secret was that the world was not separated, but was instead one interconnected piece. And that by bending his path, Max could tap into the power of the universe and become a force for good.

Max left the cave, feeling like a different person. He had unlocked the ancient secret, and he was now a true Path Bender. And he knew that he would use his powers for good, to help make the world a better place.

PART THREE
CREATING YOUR
REALITY

BECOME A PATH
BENDER TODAY

https://assemblyofwanderers.com/path-bender

CHAPTER 11: MASTERING THE RECEIVING MODE

Believe In Yourself Or Else

Max had always thought of himself as a normal person, just trying to make his way in the world. He had never heard of the legends of Path Benders, let alone believed that he was one. But after stumbling upon the mechanized cave and unlocking the ancient secret, everything changed.

He emerged from the cave, feeling like a different person. He had a newfound confidence and a sense of purpose. Max was determined to use his powers for good, to help make the world a better place.

But that newfound purpose was quickly threatened by the Agents of The System. They were determined to keep the secret of Path Bending from the public, and saw Max as a threat to their control. They wanted him dead.

Max was greatly outnumbered and, at first, struggled against the Main Agent of the System, the villain, simply now as The Captain, who was determined to take him down. Despite his best efforts, Max lost the first few battles. He simply didn't believe that he was the chosen one, or that he had the ability to bend his path. He had never seen it done before, and it all seemed too unbelievable.

But with each defeat, Max's belief in himself grew stronger. He began to see himself as the last Path Bender, and he was determined to use his powers for good. And as he continued to fight against the Agents of The System, his abilities began to grow stronger and more refined. He learned to believe in himself, and in his abilities, and with each victory, his confidence grew.

Finally, Max faced off against the the Captain in a final showdown. But he lost. He didn't believe in his path. He didn't believe in the prophecy. He barely escaped the cave alive.

Mastering the Receiving Mode

The concept of "Mastering the Receiving Mode" refers to the process of becoming open and receptive to the abundance and opportunities that the universe has to offer. It is a mindset shift from one of scarcity and fear to one of abundance and trust. By mastering the receiving mode, individuals can tap into the limitless possibilities of the universe and attract the things they desire into their lives.

The receiving mode is a state of being in which one is open to receiving love, joy, abundance, and all the good things that life has to offer. It is about letting go of limiting beliefs and expectations and becoming a blank canvas, open to receiving the gifts of the universe. The process of mastering the receiving mode requires a deep understanding of oneself and the power of the mind to create reality.

One of the key elements of mastering the receiving mode is to cultivate a positive and trusting attitude towards the universe. This means that one must believe that the universe is abundant and has endless resources and opportunities to offer. By having faith in the universe, one is able to attract the things they desire into their lives and align with the flow of life.

Another key element of mastering the receiving mode is to let go of control. This means letting go of the need to control outcomes and instead trust that the universe has a plan for us. By embracing a more relaxed and open mindset, one is able to receive what the universe has to offer without resistance.

Finally, mastering the receiving mode requires a practice of gratitude and appreciation. By focusing on the things we have and expressing gratitude for them, we are able to attract even more abundance and joy into our lives. It is a powerful tool for creating a life filled with abundance and joy.

Mastering the receiving mode is about becoming open and receptive to the gifts of the universe. It requires a positive and trusting attitude, letting go of control, and a practice of gratitude and appreciation. By mastering the receiving mode, individuals can tap into the limitless possibilities of the universe and attract the things they desire into their lives.

Mastering the Receiving Mode

The concept of "Mastering the Receiving Mode" refers to the process of becoming open and receptive to the abundance and opportunities that the universe has to offer. It is a mindset shift from one of scarcity and fear to one of abundance and trust. By mastering the receiving mode, individuals can tap into the limitless possibilities of the universe and attract the things they desire into their lives.

The receiving mode is a state of being in which one is open to receiving love, joy, abundance, and all the good things that life has to offer. It is about letting go of limiting beliefs and expectations and becoming a blank canvas, open to receiving the gifts of the universe. The process of mastering the receiving mode requires a deep understanding of oneself and the power of the mind to create reality.

One of the key elements of mastering the receiving mode is to cultivate a positive and trusting attitude towards the universe. This means that one must believe that the universe is abundant and has endless resources and opportunities to offer. By having faith in the universe, one is able to attract the things they desire into their lives and align with the flow of life.

Another key element of mastering the receiving mode is to let go of control. This means letting go of the need to control outcomes and instead trust that the universe has a plan for us. By embracing a more relaxed and open mindset, one is able to receive what the universe has to offer without resistance.

Finally, mastering the receiving mode requires a practice of gratitude and appreciation. By focusing on the things we have and expressing gratitude for them, we are able to attract even more abundance and joy into our lives. It is a powerful tool for creating a life filled with abundance and joy.

In conclusion, mastering the receiving mode is about becoming open and receptive to the gifts of the universe. It requires a positive and trusting attitude, letting go of control, and a practice of gratitude and appreciation. By mastering the receiving mode, individuals can tap into the limitless possibilities of the universe and attract the things they desire into their lives.

The Art of Vibration - Manifesting through Energy

Have you ever wondered why some people seem to attract abundance and success effortlessly, while others struggle to manifest even their most basic desires? The secret to manifestation lies in the art of vibration. The idea is simple: everything in the universe is made up of energy and everything vibrates at a certain frequency. Our thoughts and emotions also have a frequency and by aligning our vibration with that of our desires, we can attract them into our lives.

In physics, the First Law of Thermodynamics states that energy can never be created or destroyed, only transformed from one form to another. This means that everything that exists in the universe, from the tiniest particles to the largest structures, is made up of energy that has always existed and will continue to exist in some form.

So, when we talk about manifesting our desires, we're not actually creating anything new, we're simply aligning our vibration with that which already exists. We are tuning into the frequency of what we want and attracting it into our reality.

The key to this process is to let go of the idea that we need to create something new or struggle to make it happen. Instead, we need to understand that everything we desire already exists in the universe, and all we have to do is align our vibration with it. This means shifting our focus from lack and scarcity to abundance and possibility.

One way to do this is through visualization and affirmations. By visualizing what we want and affirming its existence, we are sending a clear message to the universe that we are open to receiving it. This helps to align our vibration with the frequency of our desire and attracts it into our lives.

Another way to align our vibration is through mindfulness and gratitude. When we focus on what we have, rather than what we lack, we raise our vibration and attract more positive experiences into our lives. This is because we are aligning with the frequency of abundance and gratitude.

The key to manifestation is understanding that everything already exists in the universe, and all we have to do is align our vibration with it. By shifting our focus from lack to abundance, visualizing our desires, and practicing gratitude, we can attract our desires into our reality and live a life filled with purpose, passion, and prosperity.

The Power of Receiving: Activating the Flow of Abundance into Your Life

The universe is abundant and full of endless possibilities, and when we exist in a vibration of receiving, we activate a powerful force that brings abundance and prosperity into our lives. The energy of receiving allows us to open ourselves up to the flow of the universe and tap into its infinite potential. When we exist in this vibration, things start flowing into our lives with ease and grace.

Receiving is a state of being that is rooted in gratitude, positivity, and an openness to the abundance of the universe. When we exist in this vibration, we are able to connect with the universe and align with the energy of abundance and prosperity. The more we practice receiving, the more we raise our frequency and connect with the energy of the universe.

The first law of thermodynamics states that energy can never be created or destroyed, only transformed from one form to another. This law also applies to the energy of abundance and prosperity. When we exist in a state of receiving, we are transforming the energy of abundance into our

lives and allowing it to flow freely. When we resist receiving, we block the flow of abundance and create a state of scarcity and lack.

In order to exist in the vibration of receiving, we must first adopt a mindset of abundance and positivity. This means that we must choose to focus on the good things in our lives and cultivate a sense of gratitude for what we already have. We must also release negative thoughts and limiting beliefs that prevent us from receiving.

In addition to adopting a positive mindset, there are also practical steps that we can take to activate the energy of receiving. These include:

•Practice gratitude: Make a daily habit of focusing on the things in your life that you are grateful for. Write them down, say them out loud, or simply focus on them in your mind.

•Affirm abundance: Repeat positive affirmations that align with the energy of abundance and prosperity. These affirmations should be positive, empowering, and focused on abundance and prosperity.

•Visualize abundance: Use visualization techniques to see yourself living in a state of abundance and prosperity. See yourself surrounded by abundance, and feel the energy of abundance flowing into your life.

•Take action: Take action towards your goals and desires, knowing that abundance and prosperity are already flowing into your life. This will help you to align with the energy of receiving and activate the flow of abundance.

By adopting a vibration of receiving and activating the flow of abundance into your life, you will be able to manifest your desires and live a life filled with prosperity, abundance, and joy. Remember, everything is already created, and all you have to do is exist in the vibration of receiving and allow the abundance of the universe to flow into your life.

CHAPTER 12: THE SIX PILLARS OF PATH BENDING

The Story of A Scar

Once upon a time, there was a young girl named Lily. She had a scar on her cheek that she was self-conscious about. Whenever she looked in the mirror, all she could see was her scar and all she felt was shame. She felt like she was different from everyone else and that everyone who looked at her would judge her based on her appearance.

Lily lived her life in fear of being judged and rejected because of her scar. She was afraid to take risks and step outside of her comfort zone because she believed that she wasn't good enough. She felt like a prisoner in her own body and in her own mind.

One day, Lily came across a book called "Path Bender." She read about how she had the power to bend her reality and create the life she desired. She learned that she could harness the power of the universe and use her mind to bend her path and change her reality. She learned that her thoughts and beliefs were shaping her reality, and that if she could change her thoughts and beliefs, she could change her reality.

Lily began to practice the techniques taught in the book and she started to notice a shift in her thinking. She started to see that her scar didn't define her, that it was just a small part of her story. She began to see the beauty in her uniqueness and started to embrace her scar. She started to see that everyone has scars, in one form or another, and that it was what made them unique and special.

As she continued to practice, Lily began to vibrate at a higher frequency and her reality began to change. People who she had thought were judging her, now saw her as an inspiring person, who had overcome adversity and was now shining brightly. She started to receive compliments and people would come to her for advice and guidance.

Lily had become a Path Bender and she had changed her reality by changing her thoughts and beliefs. She realized that she didn't need to create anything new, she simply had to change her vibration to align with what she desired. And that's what she did. She went from feeling like a prisoner in her own body and mind to feeling free, empowered and at peace.

Her scar was no longer a source of shame and embarrassment, but a symbol of her strength and resilience. She had learned that the most important thing was not what was on the outside, but what was on the inside. She had learned to see herself as she truly was and to love herself unconditionally.

And so, Lily's story reminds us that we all have the power to bend our path and create the life we desire. That we are all Path Benders, capable of harnessing the power of the universe and using our minds to change our reality. All we need to do is believe in ourselves, change our thoughts and beliefs, and let go of what holds us back. And just like Lily, we too can transform our lives and create a reality filled with love, joy, and abundance.

The Power of Thoughts and Feelings

In the journey of becoming a Path Bender, it is essential to understand the significance of our thoughts and feelings in shaping our experiences. Our thoughts and emotions are powerful forces that have the ability to impact our reality in profound ways.

Many of us have been taught that our external experiences are determined by external factors such as luck, fate, or circumstances beyond our control. But the truth is that our experiences are largely shaped by our internal state of mind. Our thoughts and feelings act as vibrational signals, broadcasting out into the universe, attracting experiences that match our frequency.

This concept is rooted in the law of attraction, which states that we attract into our lives whatever we focus on, believe in, and feel. If we focus on negativity, fear, and worry, we attract negative experiences into our lives. On the other hand, if we focus on positivity, love, and gratitude, we attract positive experiences.

As Path Benders, we have the power to change our thoughts and feelings and align them with our desires. By doing so, we can tap into the infinite power of the universe and manifest the experiences we want in our lives. By cultivating a positive mindset, we can raise our vibration, attract positive experiences, and live a life filled with joy, abundance, and purpose.

It is also important to understand that our feelings and emotions are not just random events, but are closely tied to our thoughts. Our feelings are the physical manifestation of our thoughts, and the more intense our thoughts, the stronger our emotions will be. This means that we can change our emotional state simply by changing our thoughts.

As Path Benders, it is crucial to recognize the immense power of our thoughts and feelings in shaping our experiences. By developing a positive mindset and cultivating a vibration of love and abundance, we can manifest a life that is filled with joy, prosperity, and purpose. Remember, the power to shape your reality is within you, and as a Path Bender, you have the tools to unlock it.

The Power of Positive Thinking: Understanding Karma as a Path Bender

As a Path Bender, it is essential to understand that your thoughts and feelings have a powerful impact on your experiences. This is why it is so important to adopt a positive and optimistic outlook on life, and to cultivate a mindset that is in alignment with your goals and desires.

One of the key principles that Path Benders understand is the idea of karma. Karma is the law of cause and effect, and it states that every action we take has a corresponding reaction. For many people, this idea is associated with negative consequences and punishments for past mistakes. However, as a Path Bender, it is important to remember that karma is never working against you, but for you.

When you approach life with a positive and optimistic mindset, you attract positive experiences and opportunities into your life. On the other hand, if you approach life with a negative and fearful mindset, you are more likely to attract negative experiences and obstacles. In other words, your thoughts and feelings act like a magnet, attracting similar experiences and outcomes into your life.

As a Path Bender, it is important to understand that your thoughts and feelings have a profound impact on your experiences and your reality. If you want to experience abundance, love, happiness, and success, you need to cultivate a mindset that is aligned with these qualities. You need to focus on what you want, rather than what you don't want. You need to adopt a vibration of abundance, and trust that the universe is working for you, not against you.

This means that you need to let go of limiting beliefs, negative self-talk, and fear-based thinking. You need to embrace change, take risks, and step outside of your comfort zone. You need to believe in yourself and your abilities, and trust that the universe will support you in your journey.

As a Path Bender, it is essential to understand that your thoughts and feelings have a powerful impact on your experiences. By embracing a positive and optimistic outlook, and by cultivating a mindset that is aligned with your goals and desires, you can tap into the power of the universe and manifest a life that is filled with purpose, passion, and prosperity. Remember, karma is never working against you, but for you, so focus on what you want, and trust that the universe will support you in your journey.

The Rise of a Young Pharaoh: A Path Bender's Journey in Ancient Egypt

Once upon a time, in ancient Egypt, there lived a young boy named Ankh. Ankh lived a simple life as a peasant in a small village along the Nile River. Despite his humble beginnings, Ankh had always felt a sense of longing for something greater. He yearned for a life filled with adventure and purpose, but he never imagined that his wildest dreams would come true.

One day, Ankh and his friends were playing in the hills surrounding their village when they stumbled upon a hidden tomb. It was said to be the final resting place of a long-forgotten pharaoh, and the entrance was guarded by two massive stone sphinxes. The children were in awe as they approached the entrance, and as they gazed upon the carvings and hieroglyphics, they noticed something strange.

Amidst the usual scenes depicting battles and offerings to the gods, there was a series of scrolls with strange markings. The children were unable to decipher the meaning, but they felt that it was important, so they took the scrolls with them and returned to the village to show their elders.

The elders were shocked and amazed by the discovery, and they quickly realized that the scrolls contained the secret to Path Bending. The art of Path Bending was thought to have been lost to time, but here it was, right in front of them. The elders tasked Ankh with the responsibility of studying the scrolls and learning the secrets of Path Bending.

Ankh threw himself into his studies, and he soon discovered that the power of Path Bending lay in the power of thought and emotion. He learned how to control his thoughts and feelings, to vibrate at the frequency of his desires, and to bend his path in order to create the reality he desired.

As Ankh grew in his abilities, he put his newfound powers to use. His village was suffering from a terrible drought that had caused crops to fail and the people to go hungry. With the power of Path Bending, Ankh was able to bend his path to bring rain to the land and save his people from starvation.

News of Ankh's feats quickly spread, and he became known as the young pharaoh who had saved a generation. He continued to use his powers for good, bringing peace and prosperity to Egypt, and his name became synonymous with Path Bending.

Years passed, and Ankh's legend grew. He became known as one of the greatest Path Benders in all of Egypt, and his story inspired generations of Egyptians to seek the power of Path Bending for themselves.

And so, the story of Ankh, the young peasant who discovered the secret to Path Bending and became a great pharaoh, lives on, a testament to the power of the mind and the ability of each of us to bend our own paths and create the reality we desire.

The Six Pillars of Path Bending: The Path to Self-Mastery

The journey of a Path Bender is not one of easy steps, but of continuous growth and self-discovery. It is a journey of transcending limitations, embracing change, and unlocking the full potential of the mind. To assist you in this journey, we have developed a powerful six-step process that has been tried and tested by Path Benders from all walks of life. This process is called The Six Pillars of Path Bending.

The Six Pillars of Path Bending is a comprehensive guide to personal transformation and self-empowerment. It provides a clear and concise framework for mastering the mind, harnessing the power of the universe, and manifesting your desires. With The Six Pillars of Path Bending, you will be able to overcome any challenge, transform your life, and achieve your goals.

The Six Pillars of Path Bending is designed to be a practical and action-oriented approach to personal growth. It provides you with the tools, techniques, and insights you need to master your thoughts, emotions, and experiences. Whether you are a beginner or an experienced Path Bender, The Six Pillars of Path Bending will provide you with the guidance and support you need to reach new heights in your journey of self-discovery.

The Six Pillars of Path Bending is a powerful process that provides a roadmap for ascending to your highest self and becoming a master of your own reality. This process is designed to help you gain a deeper understanding of yourself, your beliefs, and the world around you, and to empower you to create the life you desire. Here are the six pillars of Path Bending:

1. Experience: This pillar involves taking the time to fully experience and understand your current thoughts, feelings, and behaviors. This means paying attention to your inner dialogue, examining your beliefs and values, and noticing how you react to different situations. It's important to understand that your experiences shape your perception of reality, so it's crucial to become aware of them.

1.1   Analyze: This pillar involves analyzing your experiences in order to gain insights into your thought patterns and behaviors. Ask yourself questions like: "What do I believe about myself?" "What do I believe about others?" "What do I believe about the world around me?" By analyzing your experiences, you can start to see patterns and uncover limiting beliefs that may be holding you back.

1.2   Understanding: This pillar involves gaining a deeper understanding of your beliefs and values. This means exploring what you truly believe about yourself, others, and the world, and considering how these beliefs shape your reality. By gaining a deeper understanding of your beliefs, you can start to identify which ones are serving you and which ones are not.

1.3   Acceptance: This pillar involves accepting your experiences and beliefs, no matter how uncomfortable or unpleasant they may be. This means acknowledging your thoughts and feelings, even if they are negative, and embracing them as a part of who you are. By accepting your experiences, you can start to release negative energy and become more open to new possibilities.

1.4   Teach: This pillar involves teaching others about the power of Path Bending and sharing what you have learned about yourself and the world. By teaching others, you can help them to become more self-aware, develop a positive mindset, and create a better future for themselves and the world.

Six. Forgive: This pillar involves forgiving yourself and others for any past hurts or mistakes. This means letting go of resentment, anger, and negative feelings, and embracing a spirit of compassion and understanding. By forgiving yourself and others, you can release negative energy and cultivate a more positive and peaceful state of mind.

By following these six pillars of Path Bending, you can ascend to your highest self and become a master of your own reality. Whether you're looking to create a new career, start a business, or simply live a more fulfilling life, the Six Pillars of Path Bending provides a roadmap for making it happen.

The Orphaned Prodigy and the Path Bending Sage

Once upon a time, there was a young prodigy named Ethan. Ethan was a child of great intelligence, with an insatiable curiosity for the world around him. Despite his exceptional abilities, Ethan was an orphan, having lost both his parents at a young age. He was taken in by a distant relative, but the older woman was unable to provide the nurturing and support that Ethan needed to thrive.

One day, Ethan met an old man named Marcus, who lived in a small cottage in the countryside. Marcus was a wise and kind man who took an instant liking to Ethan. The two of them soon became fast friends, and Ethan would often visit Marcus to listen to his stories and learn from his wisdom.

One day, while they were sitting by the fire in Marcus's cottage, the old man told Ethan about a powerful process that could change his life. This process was called The Six Pillars of Path Bending, and Marcus claimed that it had the power to help Ethan understand the world around him, find his place in it, and create a life that was filled with purpose and joy.

Ethan was fascinated by the idea of Path Bending and asked Marcus to teach him. Marcus agreed and over the next few months, he showed Ethan each of the six pillars. With each lesson, Ethan grew in wisdom and understanding, and he felt his life becoming more and more aligned with his true purpose.

As Ethan learned the ways of Path Bending, he came to understand that his life was not just a series of random events, but rather a journey that was shaped by his thoughts, feelings, and beliefs. He realized that he had the power to shape his reality and create the life that he wanted, simply by changing the way that he thought and felt about it.

Ethan's journey with The Six Pillars of Path Bending was a transformative one. He went from being a lost and lonely child, to a young man who was filled with purpose and direction. He used the knowledge that he had gained to help others and create a better world for all. And so, he went on to become a teacher of The Six Pillars, passing on the wisdom that Marcus had given to him, to others who were searching for a way to understand and improve their lives.

Through his journey, Ethan came to understand that the key to living a fulfilling life was not just in acquiring knowledge, but in putting it into practice. He learned that the most important lesson of all was to always be open to new ideas, to question the status quo, and to have the courage to forge a new path in life. And so, Ethan went on to become a shining example of the power of The Six Pillars of Path Bending, a true master of his own reality.

CHAPTER 13: PATH BENDERS ARE TEACHERS

The Power of Focusing on What You Want

Have you ever found yourself constantly trying to fix or change something in your life, but no matter what you do, nothing seems to change? It's a common struggle, but the truth is that changing things on the outside won't bring lasting happiness or satisfaction. In order to create the life you truly desire, you need to change your focus.

The Path Bender philosophy stresses that what you focus on, you attract. If you constantly focus on what you don't have or what you don't like about your life, you'll only attract more of the same. If you want something new, you need to focus on what you do want.

Think about it like this: if you want a new car, you don't go around complaining about how much you hate your old car. Instead, you focus on the new car you want, you research it, and you visualize yourself driving it.

You get excited about the new car, and before you know it, you're behind the wheel of a brand new one.

It's the same with your life. If you want a new reality, don't focus on what you don't want, but create the new reality you do want. Visualize it, feel it, and most importantly, believe in it. When you focus on what you want, you start to attract it into your life.

So, if you're feeling stuck or dissatisfied with your life, try shifting your focus. Instead of trying to change what you don't like, focus on what you do want. Start visualizing and feeling your perfect reality, and watch as it begins to manifest in your life. Remember, you are the creator of your reality, and you have the power to shape it in any way you choose. So choose wisely, and always focus on what you want.

The Duty of a Path Bender: Spreading the Path Bending Message

As a Path Bender, you have a unique gift and a unique responsibility. You have the ability to shape your reality and create a life that aligns with your purpose, passion, and prosperity. However, this ability comes with a responsibility to share the knowledge and the skills that you have learned. By teaching others how to bend their own paths, you are helping them to awaken to the power of their own minds and the infinite potential of the universe.

The first step in fulfilling your duty as a Path Bender is to understand that you are not alone. There are many people in the world who are searching for their true purpose, who are feeling trapped in a reality that doesn't align with their desires. By sharing your own story and your own experiences, you can help these people to see that they too have the power to shape their own destiny.

The second step is to be an example. The best way to teach others how to bend their paths is to lead by example. This means that you must live your life as a Path Bender, and be a shining light for others to follow. Your actions and your words should reflect the values and the principles of Path Bending, and inspire others to take the leap and start bending their own paths.

The third step is to provide guidance and support. This means that you must be willing to answer questions, offer advice, and provide resources that can help others to bend their paths. You may also want to consider forming a community of Path Benders, where you can share your experiences, offer support to each other, and work together to spread the message of Path Bending to the world.

The fourth step is to be patient and persistent. The process of Path Bending is not always easy, and it can take time for others to see the results of their efforts. However, as a Path Bender, you must have the patience and persistence to continue to share the message, and to help others to stay focused on their goals.

The final step is to have a clear understanding of your purpose. As a Path Bender, your purpose is not just to live a life of purpose, passion, and prosperity, but also to help others to do the same. When you understand your purpose, you will be able to inspire others with your passion and your enthusiasm, and help them to see that they too can bend their paths and create the lives of their dreams.

The duty of a Path Bender is to share the message of Path Bending with others. By helping others to bend their own paths, you are spreading the message of hope, of possibility, and of infinite potential. And as more and more people start to bend their paths, the world will become a better place, filled with more happiness, more joy, and more love.

The Legacy of the Path Bender: A Tale of Wealth and Wisdom

Once upon a time, in a small village nestled in the mountains, lived an old man named Jonas. Jonas was a wealthy man, but unlike many wealthy people, he did not spend his money on frivolous things. Instead, he lived a simple life and spent his days studying and contemplating the world around him.

As he grew older, Jonas became more and more aware of the immense power of the mind and how it could shape one's reality. He knew that he could not take his wealth with him when he died, so he made a decision. He would give away his entire fortune to someone who had the true heart of a Path Bender.

Years went by and Jonas continued to live a simple life. He would often watch the villagers as they went about their daily lives and would listen to their stories. But, no matter how hard he looked, he could not find anyone who possessed the qualities of a Path Bender.

One day, a young boy came to the village. His name was Matthew and he was an orphan. Matthew was a kind and curious boy, always eager to learn and help others. Jonas took an immediate liking to him and took him under his wing.

Over the years, Jonas taught Matthew about the world, about the power of the mind, and about Path Bending. He showed him how to see the world from a different perspective and how to use his thoughts and feelings to shape his reality. Matthew was a quick learner and soon became a master of Path Bending himself.

When Jonas grew old and knew that his time was coming to an end, he called Matthew to his side. He told Matthew that he had found the true heart of a Path Bender and that he was leaving his entire fortune to him.

Matthew was stunned. He could not believe that Jonas would give him everything he had worked for his entire life. But, Jonas told him that he had seen the love and kindness in Matthew's heart and knew that he would use his wealth for the good of others.

Matthew became a wealthy man, but he never forgot the lessons that Jonas had taught him. He used his wealth to help others and to spread the teachings of Path Bending. He became known as one of the greatest Path Benders of all time, and people from all over the world came to him for guidance.

Years went by, and Matthew grew old and died. But, his legacy lived on, as people continued to study the teachings of Path Bending and use them to shape their own realities. And, just like Jonas, Matthew left his wealth to someone who had the true heart of a Path Bender, ensuring that the teachings would continue to be passed down for generations to come.

Forgiving at a Higher Level: The Path Bender's Way

Forgiveness is a critical component of the Path Bender's journey. Path Benders understand that forgiveness is not just about letting go of resentment and anger towards others, but also about letting go of negative thoughts and beliefs about themselves. They understand that holding onto grudges and negative feelings only serve to weigh them down, prevent growth, and hold them back from manifesting the life they truly desire.

Path Benders forgive at a higher level because they recognize that everyone is doing the best they can with the resources they have. They understand that everyone is on their own journey and that their actions and decisions are a reflection of their current state of being. Path Benders do not judge others for their actions, but instead strive to understand and empathize with them.

Forgiveness is also a key component of the Path Bender's ability to manifest the life they desire. By letting go of negative feelings and beliefs, they free up mental and emotional energy, which allows them to focus on what they want to create in their life. This focus, combined with the vibration of forgiveness, attracts positive experiences, opportunities, and relationships into their life.

Path Benders are also able to forgive themselves. They understand that they are human and that they make mistakes. Instead of beating themselves up or dwelling on their past failures, they choose to forgive themselves and use those experiences as opportunities for growth and learning.

Path Benders forgive at a higher level because they understand that everyone is doing the best they can and that holding onto negative feelings only serves to weigh them down. They are able to forgive themselves and others, which allows them to free up mental and emotional energy to focus on what they want to create in their life. By embodying the vibration of forgiveness, they are able to manifest a life filled with love, abundance, and joy.

Forgiveness Beyond the Veil: A Path Bender's Journey

Once upon a time, there was a middle-aged woman named Sarah who lived a simple life in the countryside. She was a kind-hearted person, always eager to help others and had a deep love for nature. One day, while she was working in her garden, she noticed a figure that seemed to be floating in the air. Sarah was frightened, as she had never seen anything like it before.

She cautiously approached the figure, and to her shock, she realized that it was the ghost of her late husband, Thomas. Sarah was filled with fear, but she also felt a strong sense of love and compassion towards

Thomas. He had been a kind and loving husband, but he had also made many mistakes in his life.

As Sarah approached Thomas, he spoke to her in a soft voice, "My dear Sarah, I need your forgiveness." Sarah was taken aback by this request. She had already forgiven Thomas for his mistakes when he was alive, but she had never considered the idea of forgiving his ghost.

But Sarah was a Path Bender, and she knew that forgiveness at a higher level was part of her duty as a Path Bender. She closed her eyes and took a deep breath, allowing herself to let go of all her anger and resentment towards Thomas. She forgave him completely, from the bottom of her heart.

As Sarah opened her eyes, she saw Thomas begin to fade away, a peaceful look on his face. He had finally found the forgiveness he needed to move on to the afterlife. Sarah watched as Thomas disappeared into the ether, feeling a deep sense of peace and joy in her heart.

From that day on, Sarah became a beacon of light, spreading the message of forgiveness to all those around her. She inspired others to follow her example and forgive at a higher level, just as she had done with Thomas. Sarah's journey as a Path Bender had led her to a new understanding of the power of forgiveness and the importance of letting go of the past. And so, her legacy lived on, guiding others to find peace and happiness in their lives through the path of forgiveness.

CHAPTER 14: A PATH BENDER'S GREATEST THREAT

Breaking Free from Regret: The Path Bender's Greatest Threat

Regret is a powerful force that can hold us back from experiencing the full potential of our lives. It is the feeling of remorse or sorrow for something that has already happened, and it can have a profound impact on our mental and emotional state. As Path Benders, it is important to understand the role that regret plays in our lives, and to take steps to overcome it.

Regret is a vibration that locks us into a reality that is unworthy of us. It is created by unresolved issues that have not been analyzed and accepted in the Six Pillars of Path Bending. When we hold onto regret, we create a blockage in our energy that keeps us from experiencing the full potential of our lives.

The good news is that Path Benders have the ability to break free from the grip of regret. By analyzing and understanding the root cause of our regrets, we can begin to release the negative energy that is holding us back. Through acceptance and forgiveness, we can create a new reality for ourselves, free from the limitations of the past.

The Six Pillars of Path Bending provide a powerful framework for breaking free from regret. By following the steps of experiencing, analyzing, understanding, accepting, teaching, and forgiving, we can clear the blockages in our energy and find peace and contentment in our lives.

So if you find yourself struggling with regret, remember that you have the power to break free. By following the Six Pillars of Path Bending, you can reclaim your power, and live a life that is full of abundance, joy, and peace.

What Is Regret?

Regret is a feeling that has been around since the beginning of human history. It is an emotion that stems from the realization that one could have done something differently in the past, and as a result, things could have turned out differently. Regret is an instinctual response that is rooted in the desire to survive and thrive in the world. In our primal days, regret served an important purpose. It was a way for our ancestors to assess their actions and avoid repeating mistakes that could lead to danger or death.

However, in the modern world, regret can have profound effects on the human mind. The feeling of regret can often linger and turn into a persistent negative thought pattern that can have a negative impact on one's mental health. Regret can cause a person to feel overwhelmed with feelings of guilt and shame, leading to low self-esteem, anxiety, and depression.

Furthermore, regret can also lead to a sense of hopelessness and a belief that it's too late to change the past. This can result in a person feeling stuck in their current reality, unable to move forward and create a better future for themselves.

In short, regret is a powerful emotion that has both positive and negative effects on the human mind. While it served an important purpose in our primal days, in the modern world, it can be a major hindrance to personal growth and well-being. For Path Benders, it is important to understand the origins of regret and its effects on the mind in order to avoid getting stuck in a negative thought pattern and continue to grow and evolve.

The Negative Impact of Regret on Desires and Dreams

Regret is a feeling that is often associated with a sense of remorse or sadness over something that was not accomplished or done differently in the past. It is a primal emotion that has a significant impact on the human mind and can ultimately prevent us from manifesting our desires and achieving our dreams.

When we experience regret, it creates a vibration that is not aligned with our desires and goals. This vibration attracts experiences that are not in line with what we want and creates an obstacle that makes it difficult to manifest our desires. Regret can also cause us to dwell on the past and distract us from focusing on the present moment and our goals.

One of the biggest impacts of regret is that it can limit our ability to think positively and be optimistic about the future. This negative mindset can prevent us from taking action towards our desires and goals and create a cycle of disappointment and dissatisfaction.

Moreover, regret can also cause us to lose faith in our ability to achieve our desires and can lead us to believe that our dreams are impossible to attain. This lack of faith and belief in oneself can have a devastating impact on our motivation and drive to succeed.

Finally, regret can also prevent us from forgiving ourselves and others. It is important to understand that forgiveness is an integral part of the Path

Bending process and is essential in order to move forward and achieve our goals. Holding on to regret and not forgiving can create an obstacle that prevents us from vibrating at a frequency that is aligned with our desires.

Regret is a powerful emotion that can have a significant impact on our ability to manifest our desires and achieve our dreams. It is important for Path Benders to understand the negative impact of regret and to work on letting go of past experiences and forgive themselves and others in order to move forward and reach their full potential.

The Eternal Weight of Regret

Once upon a time, there was a young woman named Sarah. She was in love with a man named Michael, and they were engaged to be married. Sarah had always dreamed of finding true love and having a family of her own, and she thought she had finally found that with Michael.

However, just a few months before the wedding, Michael suddenly broke up with Sarah. He claimed that he just wasn't ready for marriage, and that he needed time to figure things out. Sarah was devastated by the sudden breakup, and she felt as if her whole world had fallen apart.

In the months that followed, Sarah found herself consumed by regret. She couldn't help but wonder what she could have done differently to keep Michael by her side. She thought about all the things she could have said or done to make him see how much she loved him, and how much they belonged together.

As the years went by, Sarah's regret only grew stronger. She never married, never had children, and never realized any of her other dreams because she was so consumed by what she had lost. She felt as if she was living in a world of "what ifs" and "if onlys", and she could never seem to escape the weight of her regret.

Eventually, Sarah grew old and died, still carrying the weight of her regret with her to the grave. She had never truly let go of her love for Michael, and she had never fully forgiven herself for what had happened between them. Her life had become a sad, lonely existence, all because of her inability to forgive and move on from her past.

The moral of Sarah's story is that regret can be a heavy burden to carry, and it can prevent us from realizing our dreams and experiencing true happiness in life. As Path Benders, it is important to forgive and let go of the things in our past that hold us back, so that we can move forward and create the lives we truly desire.

The Only Moment That Matters

The second law of thermodynamics states that entropy, or the measure of disorder in a system, always increases over time. This means that everything in the universe is moving towards a state of greater disorder and randomness. And so, in this sense, we can never go back and "fix" anything that has already happened in the past.

However, what's more important to focus on is the fact that time itself is an illusion. Yes, we experience it, but time is simply a construct created by our minds to give us a sense of order and structure in our lives. In reality, there is no past, present, or future. All that exists is the present moment.

So, what does this mean for us as Path Benders? It means that we need to stop dwelling on the past and worrying about the future. The only moment that matters is now. If you're feeling regret or longing for something that has already happened, remind yourself that it's not real. The past is gone and the future is not here yet. All you have is the present moment, and it's up to you to make the most of it.

It's also important to understand that your thoughts and feelings about the past can impact your present experiences. If you hold onto regret, it can prevent you from moving forward and reaching your desires. On the other hand, if you let go of regret and focus on the present moment, you'll be able to vibrate at a higher frequency and manifest the life you truly want.

So, as a Path Bender, remember that the past is gone and the future is not here yet. All you have is the present moment, and it's up to you to make the most of it. Focus on the present and don't let regret hold you back. The only moment that matters is now.

Regret is a powerful force that can take hold of us and control our lives. It is a vibration that locks us into a reality that is unworthy of us, and it comes from unresolved issues that have not been analyzed and accepted through the Six Pillars of Path Bending.

But despite the negative impact of regret on our desires and dreams, it is important to remember that we always have the power to choose our thoughts and feelings in each moment. And as Path Benders, we have a special responsibility to forgive ourselves and others, and to let go of the past.

The truth is, you can never go back and fix anything. The second law of thermodynamics won't allow it, and time is an illusion. But in our illusion, all we have is the present moment, and it is in this moment that we have the power to change our vibration and attract a new reality.

So instead of dwelling on what could have been, let's focus on what can be. Let's focus on our desires and dreams, and let's believe in our ability to manifest them into reality.

And above all, let's remember that we are all perfect, exactly as we are. Our experiences, both good and bad, are perfect too. They are here to teach us, to help us grow, and to lead us to where we need to be.

So let's choose to forgive ourselves and others, to let go of regret, and to live in the vibration of receiving. Let's choose to be Path Benders, and let's create the reality we truly deserve.

The journey of Path Bending may not always be easy, but the rewards are immeasurable. It empowers us to live life with purpose, intention, and abundance. So, let us choose to rise above regret and embrace the power of the present moment, for this is the only moment we truly have. This is where our power lies, and where our greatest potential for growth and happiness lies. Remember, as Path Benders, we have the power to bend our own path, and to live a life filled with joy, abundance, and purpose.

PART FOUR
BECOMING A
PATH BENDER

BECOME A PATH BENDER TODAY

https://assemblyofwanderers.com/path-bender

CHAPTER 15: LOVE AND LIGHT: THE HEARTBEAT OF A PATH BENDER

In the path of a Path Bender, the understanding of love and light is of utmost importance. Love and light are not just words or concepts, but they are the foundation and the source of power for the Path Bender's journey. According to the teachings of Ra, love and light are the enabler, the power, and the energy giver. They are the manifestation of the union of love and light in the manifestation of creation.

The concept of love and light can be seen as a vibration or density that is the result of the impressed love on light. It is a manifestation of the understanding of love and its application in the world. Love is the great activator and primal co-Creator of various creations using intelligent infinity. Love, in its essence, is an activity called "loving" without significant distortion. Path Benders who have learned to do this activity seek the ways of light or wisdom.

In vibratory sense, love comes into light as the activity of unity in its free will. Love uses light and has the power to direct light in its distortions. This is why vibratory complexes in a Path Bender's journey recapitulate in reverse the creation in its unity, showing the rhythm or flow of the great heartbeat.

Love and light are not just concepts or ideas, but they are the manifestation of the Path Bender's true nature and the source of their power. By embracing love and light in their journey, Path Benders create a reality that is harmonious and filled with peace. They are the beating heart of the Path Bender's journey, and by understanding and embracing their true nature, they create a reality that is worthy of them.

The Unexpected Fortune of Love and Light

Once upon a time, there was a young boy named Timmy who lived in a small village on the outskirts of the city. Timmy's family was poor, and they lived in a tiny shack with a leaky roof and no heat in the winter. Despite these difficulties, Timmy was a happy child, always smiling and playing with his friends.

One day, Timmy was playing in the village square when he stumbled upon a large, rusty old chest. Being a curious child, he opened the chest, and to his surprise, he found a massive pile of gold coins inside. Timmy couldn't believe his luck! He had never seen so much money in his life.

Overwhelmed with joy, Timmy ran home to tell his family the good news. They were all shocked and couldn't believe that Timmy had come into an unexpected fortune. They quickly used the money to improve their living conditions and buy food, clothing, and other necessities.

But Timmy knew that he couldn't just keep the money for himself. He had learned about the Law of One, which was the balancing of love/light and light/love. Love/light was the enabler, the power, the energy giver. Light/love was the manifestation which occurred when light had been impressed with love.

Timmy understood that he had to use his newfound wealth to help others. He started by donating money to the village's food bank, and then he helped to rebuild the homes of those who were less fortunate. His actions inspired others to do the same, and soon the entire village was filled with love and light.

Timmy's heart was filled with the vibration of love, and he continued to spread it to everyone he met. He had learned to do an activity called "loving" without significant distortion, and he sought the ways of light and wisdom. In doing so, he had become a true Path Bender.

And as he continued on his journey, he came to understand that love is the great activator and primal co-Creator of various creations using intelligent infinity. He learned that love uses light and has the power to direct light in its distortions, and that love's vibration recapitulates in reverse the creation in its unity, showing the rhythm or flow of the great heartbeat.

Timmy lived the rest of his life spreading love and light to everyone he met, and he was remembered as a true Path Bender who had used his unexpected fortune to change the world. And so, Timmy's story lives on as a testament to the power of love and the impact it can have on the world when it is used in the right way.

The Flow of Love and the Path Benders

The flow of love is a concept that is central to the teachings of the Path Benders. It is believed that love, in its purest form, is the life force that energizes and sustains all things. This love is a creative force, originating from the One Infinite, and streaming into the individual through a web of electromagnetic points or link of entrance.

The Path Benders understand that these points are like portals, allowing the love/light energy to enter the individual and bring life to their being. This energy is then available to the individual, providing them with the power to bring love and light into their lives and into the lives of those around them.

In order for this flow of love to remain balanced and free-flowing, the Path Benders teach that individuals must work to maintain balance in their own energy centers. They must also strive to overcome the blockages that may exist within their own mind, body, and spirit. This requires a commitment to personal growth and a willingness to embrace love and light in all aspects of one's life.

The Path Benders play a vital role in facilitating this flow of love. Through their teachings and guidance, they help individuals to understand the nature of this energy and how it can be harnessed and utilized to bring greater balance, peace, and fulfillment into their lives. They also work to help individuals overcome the blockages that may prevent the flow of love, and to foster a greater sense of unity and connection with the One Infinite.

In this way, the Path Benders are an important part of the flow of love, working to bring greater balance, love, and light into the world. They provide individuals with the tools and understanding needed to become a conduit for this energy, and to bring love and light into their own lives and into the lives of others. And in doing so, they help to create a brighter and more harmonious world for all.

The Triad of Light, Love, and Free Will

In the teachings of Path Benders, it is believed that there are only three fundamental forces that exist in the world. These three forces are Light, Love, and Free Will. Each of these three things is the original vibration of this planetary illusion and together they form a powerful triad that creates, shapes, and determines the nature of reality.

Light is the energy that creates all things. It is the source of life and the foundation upon which everything is built. Light is the energy that animates and sustains the world, and without it, there would be no life. The Path Benders believe that the source of light is the One Infinite, and that this light streams into the planetary sphere through the electromagnetic web of points or nexi of entrance.

Love is the force that shapes the light into what it will become. It is the power that imbues the light with meaning and purpose. Love is what gives light its direction and meaning, and it is what creates the patterns and structures of the world. The Path Benders believe that love is the co-

Creator of reality and that it works hand in hand with light to bring the world into being.

Free Will is the final piece of the triad, and it determines how we will interact with others and the world around us. It is the power that gives us the ability to choose and to act, and it is what makes us truly free. The Path Benders believe that Free Will is the key to unlocking the full potential of the light and love that exist within us. With Free Will, we can choose to use the light and love in a positive and productive way, or we can choose to ignore it and live a life of darkness and fear.

Path Benders believe that the Triad of Light, Love, and Free Will is the foundation of reality, and that by understanding and embracing these three forces, we can create a better and more harmonious world. The Path Benders seek to understand and harness the power of this triad, so that they can use it to bring peace and happiness to the world. They believe that by following this path, they can help to create a world where love and light are the guiding forces, and where free will is the key to unlocking our full potential.

Path Benders And The Journey of The Soul

In the teachings of the Path Benders, all things are one, and all beings are connected and that all lives are part of the same cosmic tapestry. This law is based on the understanding that there is only one Source of energy in this world, which is light. This light is transformed into different forms through love, and the free will of individuals determines how this light will be interacted with and utilized.

As individuals complete their cycles of experience, they demonstrate different degrees of understanding and distortions of their individual Hero's Journey. This leads to a separation of individuals into different vibrational frequencies, each suited to their own experiences of what they call life.

The journey of the soul is guided by nurturing beings who are close to Path Benders in their own distortions but have a desire for active service and service to others. The journey begins with the spirit complex, as *The Law of One* would call it, moving along a line of light, until it becomes too intense and the entity stops. This is the point at which the entity reaches the end of the third-density light/love distortion and begins a major cycle of discovery and growth.

The cycle is an opportunity for individuals to discover the distortions that are inherent in themselves and to work towards reducing these distortions. Through this journey, individuals grow closer to the idea of *Everything Is Perfect*, and in doing so, they become more aligned with the greater cosmic tapestry. This journey is a central part of the Path Benders' teachings and is considered essential for reaching a deeper understanding of the universe and one's place within it.

The One Infinite Creator

The Path Benders believe in the existence of a single and all-encompassing entity that created everything in existence. This entity is referred to as the One Infinite Creator. The One Infinite Creator is the source of all light, love, and life in the universe. This idea is a fundamental belief of the Path Benders, as they understand that everything that exists is a manifestation of the One Infinite Creator.

In a teleological sense, the One Infinite Creator is the origin of all things and is the only entity that truly exists. The One Infinite Creator can be seen as the `seed-form of everything in existence, from which everything else manifests. This concept is not easily understood by the physical mind, as it is difficult to grasp the idea of a single entity that is both infinite and all-encompassing.

However, for those who seek to understand the Path Benders' teachings, the concept of the One Infinite Creator is of great importance. Through the practice of love and light, the Path Benders believe that they can come to understand the One Infinite Creator and live in harmony with its laws. By embracing the limitless light of the One Infinite Creator, they can grow and evolve, becoming more attuned to the true nature of existence.

The Path Benders believe that the One Infinite Creator is the origin of all things and that its light, love, and life are the driving forces behind existence. By embracing these principles and seeking to understand the One Infinite Creator, they believe that they can live in harmony with the universe and achieve a greater understanding of the nature of existence.

CHAPTER 16: UNDERSTANDING THIS ILLUSION

Graduation and the Three-Way Split

In the Path of Benders, it is believed that all beings will eventually reach a point in their journey where they must graduate to the next level of existence. This graduation is known as the three-way split, where entities will either continue their journey on this plane in fourth-density experience, move on to another planet for a negative polarity harvest, or continue their journey on another third-density planet.

The beings that make up this graduation come from different parts of the universe, including those that have been on the planet Earth for many incarnations, those that have come to Earth specifically to transition into fourth density, and Wanderers who have come to this plane for their own reasons.

It is a complex process, but the Path Benders understand that it is a natural part of the journey of all beings. The split allows for growth, discovery, and the opportunity to move forward in one's evolution. The Path Benders see themselves as guides and nurturers, helping entities to make the transition to the next stage with grace and understanding.

The Path Benders believe that all entities have the power of free will, and it is this power that will determine their path during the three-way split. Whether one continues on the path of light and love, or chooses another path, the Path Benders believe that the journey will ultimately lead to a greater understanding of the One Infinite Creator.

So What Are Densities?

The Path Benders philosophy is centered around the concept of light and how it shapes our understanding of the world. In this chapter, we will discuss what density is and how it relates to light and consciousness.

Density refers to the amount of energy (or information) that is contained within a given space. The connectedness of information is what determines the density of a space. As the connectedness increases, the density of the space also increases, allowing for more information to be experienced.

It is important to understand the densities of light, as they are also referred to as the densities of consciousness. Each density represents a different level of vibration and awareness, allowing for a greater understanding of the world and the beings within it. By understanding the powers and limitations of each energy level, we can better understand the world around us, as well as our own evolution as a species.

The Path Benders view the densities of light as the lessons that we must learn in order to progress and evolve as conscious beings. These lessons range from learning to love and understand others, to understanding the interconnectedness of all things.

The densities of light play a crucial role in the Path Benders philosophy. They represent the journey of consciousness and understanding, and provide insight into the workings of the universe and our place within it.

First Density - The Consciousness of Simple Existence

In Path Benders, we explore the densities of light, or the densities of consciousness. The first density, also known as 1D, represents the root chakra and is associated with the color red. This density represents the weaving of light into physical reality, through atoms and their interactions. The first density includes the primal configurations of energy structures and can be seen in the structural possibilities of atoms, including molecules, lattices, and larger fractal atomic structures like the physical structure of galaxies.

1D can be visualized as a torus connected in strings. The conscious experience of 1D is expression, resonation, and crystallization. For the manifestation of the higher densities, they must go down and down, and the most powerful manifestations reach all the way to this density, merging with the first density consciousness of atoms and other tight forms of light.

Examples of 1D include crystals, rocks, fire, wind, electricity, and water (the elements). The lesson of 1D is the existence as duality: oneness (through resonance) and separation through experiencing the push and pull (yin and yang) that makes physical reality possible.

In terms of consciousness, 1D corresponds to physical matter, its states – solid, liquid, gas, etc – the archetypical elements – air, water, soil, fire – and the chemical substances matter is composed of – Oxygen, Hydrogen, etc. If our consciousness were to be at the 1D level, our point of focus would be the electron, the proton, the molecule, and the energies between them.

In conclusion, 1D represents the beginning of our journey through the densities of light and consciousness. It is the foundation upon which the higher densities are built and is essential to understanding our place in the universe. Through a deeper understanding of 1D, we can better comprehend our connection to the physical world and the manifestation of consciousness in the material realm.

Understanding Second Density

In Path Benders, we explore the various densities of consciousness that exist within our physical reality. The second density, represented by the sacral chakra and the color orange, encompasses the realm of "animated" consciousness. This includes all forms of life, starting from the single-cell level, that engage and interact with their environment and with each other.

The visual representation of second density is a fractal tree, a physical skeleton of a torus that symbolizes any energy system, whether it be a human, a planet, or a plant. The conscious experience of second density is about receiving plenty from the source and growing into a unique personality through physical form and movement.

Examples of second density include plants, animal life, fungi, trees, fruits, and vegetables. Pets, being high or late second density, are also part of this realm of consciousness. The lesson of second density is centered around growth towards the source, on Earth represented by the Sun, and movement through awareness.

In second density, consciousness grows towards the infinite oneness, expanding like a tree growing towards the Sun. This growth is an important step in the journey towards higher densities, where beings can experience more complex states of awareness and consciousness. Understanding second density allows us to appreciate the interconnectedness of all life and the role it plays in our physical reality.

Third Density - Self-Awareness (This Is Where You Are Reading This Book)

The Third Density, represented by the Solar Plexus Chakra with the color Yellow or Golden, is a level of consciousness where self-awareness emerges. This density is characterized by the presence of decisions, choices, and self-identification.

At the 3D level, entities have the ability to create a conceptualization of the world around them and make decisions based on this understanding. This ability to judge value, to distinguish between right and wrong, is a unique trait of the Third Density. This dualistic judgement, although simplistic, is the basis for making choices.

The main goal of the Third Density is to learn the ways of love. The time it takes to move through the first and second densities can be millions or billions of years, but the Third Density is approximately 75,000 years long. Unlike the other densities, the Third Density has more catalyst, which forces entities to deal with each other in such a way as to involve love and growth in spirituality.

Third Density consciousness is where human beings live now. It is the Density of free-will, where entities have the power to make choices and decisions based on their beliefs. However, this freedom to make choices can also lead to a perception of "every man for himself", which can result in negative choices that cause much separation and pain.

The visual representation of the Third Density is a Fractal Tree consciously deciding which branch to grow further. The conscious experience of this density is self-identification, expression, and choices. The Third Density is exemplified by humans, but some believe that playful, socializing animals like dolphins and manatees are also part of this density.

The lesson of the Third Density is choice. In this density, entities have the opportunity to learn and grow through their choices and decisions, and ultimately, to learn the ways of love.

Harmonious Relationships and Service to Others in Path Benders

As beings progress on their spiritual journey, they come to understand the energies that have created the minds, bodies, and spirits of entities in their environment. These energies include both natural and man-made influences. It is important to recognize the importance of the energy of love and light in the creation of the spiritual being.

One of the key areas to focus on is the consideration of the needs of both the natural environment and the needs of other beings. Each entity is unique and what may be seen as an improper distortion for one, may not be for another. Therefore, it is important to become aware of the other-self as self and to act in a way that is in accordance with their needs, understanding from their perspective.

This process of service and compassion requires sensitivity and an ability to empathize. It is important to understand that sometimes the breaking of the distortion of free will may not be necessary and it is a delicate matter to navigate.

The societal complex is an arena where the entities have a duty to act according to their free will for the benefit of the social complex. There are two simple directives in this area: awareness of the intelligent energy expressed in nature, and awareness of the intelligent energy expressed in oneself, to be shared when appropriate with the social complex.

It is important to note that while focusing on harmonious relationships and service to others, the emphasis should not be on infringing on one's free will, but rather, on finding a balance between self and others for mutual benefit. The subtleties in this arena are infinite, and it is up to each entity to navigate them with care and awareness.

The journey towards harmonious relationships and service to others is one that requires sensitivity, empathy, and a deep understanding of the needs of both self and others. The focus should be on creating a balance that benefits all, without infringing on the free will of any entity.

Exploring the Fourth Density

As we journey further along the spiritual path, we come to the fourth density, a realm of consciousness characterized by love, compassion, and harmony. This density is represented by the heart chakra, which is often associated with the color green or pink.

In fourth density, we are able to connect with the essence of things, transcending the boundaries of time and space. This allows us to interact with the entire past and future of a phenomenon through the present moment, and to directly influence the past and future through the power of our thoughts and emotions.

The conscious experience of fourth density is one of overwhelming love and a deep understanding of the interconnectedness of all things. Thoughts are transparent and communication is possible without the use of words, leading to a feeling of unity and oneness with all life. Physical bodies are still present in this density, but the lifespan of a 4D being is 90,000 Earth years, with an expected stay of about 30 million years.

The lesson of fourth density is love. This is the consciousness of empathy and compassion, where the importance of living in harmony with others and avoiding harm to others is emphasized. On this level, the spiritual, esoteric, and energy aspects of reality are no longer questioned, but are accepted as intrinsic parts of existence, regardless of whether they are fully understood or not.

The path to fourth density is a journey of self-discovery, where we learn to love ourselves and to extend that love to others. As we cultivate compassion and empathy, we learn to appreciate the beauty and interconnectedness of all things, and to live in harmony with others and the natural world.

So, as we venture into the realm of fourth density, let us embrace the journey with open hearts and a deep sense of love and compassion for all life.

Exploring the Fifth Density

In 5th density, represented by the Throat Chakra, Color Blue, individuals are able to connect with their own unique and individual essence and truth, while still recognizing the interconnectedness of all things. This allows them to explore and express their own individuality while still remaining in harmony with the universe. The life span of a 5th density being is 150,000 earth years and they can expect to remain in this density for approximately 60,000 million years.

In 5D, the focus is on exploring the inner connection to Intelligent Infinity and one's own intrinsic nature and essence. The physical bodies become malleable and entities can easily traverse and mold time and space through thought and energy. This is the last density where physical matter exists and marks the boundary between the realms of solid matter and those of pure subtle energy, which are used by souls for the exploration of consciousness.

The lesson of 5th density is wisdom. By connecting with their own truth and individuality, individuals in 5th density gain a deeper understanding and connection with the universe. Through this, they are able to access wisdom and insight that transcends time and space.

In 5D, the focus becomes less on the relationship and interactions with others and more on exploring the inner connection to Intelligent Infinity and one's own intrinsic nature and essence. This allows individuals to evolve and grow, ultimately leading to a deeper understanding of the universe and their place within it.

At 7th density, all illusions of separation and duality are dissolved, and a being becomes fully integrated with the Infinite Void. This is the density of pure consciousness, where the concept of "self" still exists but only as a fleeting thought within the vast expanse of infinite consciousness.

A being at 7th density is a master of all lessons learned throughout their journey through the densities and has fully realized the true nature of reality as pure consciousness. They no longer have a need to seek out lessons or experiences as they have fully integrated all aspects of themselves.

In 7th density, there is no duality, no positive or negative, only pure consciousness and infinite potential for expression. The crown chakra, represented by the color violet, is fully opened and a being at this density has a connection to the Infinite Void and all possibilities.

A being at 7th density is considered an oversoul, and serves as a source of guidance and wisdom for beings at lower densities. They are fully in tune with the larger consciousness and see themselves as a part of the greater whole, while still retaining their individual consciousness.

The lesson of 7th density is completion, the realization that all experiences and lessons are part of a larger journey, and the ultimate merging with the Infinite Void. This density represents the end of the journey through the densities, and the beginning of a new cycle, where a being has the potential to start anew and continue their evolution.

In the realm of Path Benders, the 6th density, represented by the Third Eye Chakra Color Indigo, is known to be the birthplace of the archangels. It is a place where individuals reach a level of consciousness that transcends dualistic beliefs and perspectives. This level of consciousness is characterized by the ability to perceive all sides of any circumstances or questions, and is referred to as overarching insight.

Graduation from 5D to 6D requires an entity to confront any remaining negativity and separation within themselves. In doing so, they recognize that all external negativity and separation is merely a reflection of their own inner negativity and separation. This realization allows individuals in 6D to integrate all opposing forces within themselves and no longer draw negativity into their own reality.

In 6D, entities still exist in shapes and forms and may hold a body based in and around planetary or celestial bodies. However, they are ultimately made of light and are unbounded from solid physical matter. At this level, entities are simultaneously individuals and part of larger collectives, and there are no definite boundaries between the external and internal.

Entities in 6D are solely focused on their spiritual tasks and interests. Their challenge is often to discern what is inner and what is outer, as only the inner is ultimately true. In 6D, there is no negative polarity, but rather, different gradations of light. These gradations determine what is considered appropriate or inappropriate for the self.

The 6D realm is considered the gateway density, and the last density before mind, body, and spirit complexes merge back into the creator. It is a place where individuals have reached a level of unity with all things, and their consciousness has evolved through eons of time. The archangels of 6D are a testament to the power of spiritual evolution and the transformative journey of Path Benders.

Exploring the Seventh Density

At 7th density, all illusions of separation and duality are dissolved, and a being becomes fully integrated with the Infinite Void. This is the density of pure consciousness, where the concept of "self" still exists but only as a fleeting thought within the vast expanse of infinite consciousness.

A being at 7th density is a master of all lessons learned throughout their journey through the densities and has fully realized the true nature of reality as pure consciousness. They no longer have a need to seek out lessons or experiences as they have fully integrated all aspects of themselves.

In 7th density, there is no duality, no positive or negative, only pure consciousness and infinite potential for expression. The crown chakra, represented by the color violet, is fully opened and a being at this density has a connection to the Infinite Void and all possibilities.

A being at 7th density is considered an oversoul, and serves as a source of guidance and wisdom for beings at lower densities. They are fully in tune with the larger consciousness and see themselves as a part of the greater whole, while still retaining their individual consciousness.

The lesson of 7th density is completion, the realization that all experiences and lessons are part of a larger journey, and the ultimate merging with the Infinite Void. This density represents the end of the journey through the densities, and the beginning of a new cycle, where a being has the potential to start anew and continue their evolution.

Exploring the Eighth Density

Represented By: No physical representation as 8D exists beyond physical form

Description: The final density where all conscious entities merge back into the Creator.

In 8D, the spiritual mass of all infinite universes converge into one central sun or Creator, resulting in the birth of a new universe, a new infinity, and a new Logos. This new Logos incorporates all that the Creator has experienced of itself through its journey across the densities.

Conscious Experience: Beyond physical form and finite experience. At 8D, all entities merge back into the infinite consciousness of the Creator.

Lesson: Reintegration with the source. The final stage in the journey of conscious evolution on this octave.

It is also mentioned that there are entities that wander in 8D, who come to aid in the completion of the Logos in our octave. However, little is known about these entities as they exist beyond our current understanding.

Visual: No physical representation exists for 8D as it exists beyond physical form.

8D represents the ultimate destination for all conscious entities. It is the density where the journey of evolution and experience come full circle, as all entities merge back into the infinite consciousness of the Creator.

CHAPTER 17: PHYSICS AND PATH BENDERS

Einstein's theory of mass-energy equivalence, famously represented by the equation E=mc^2, is a cornerstone of modern physics and provides a deep insight into the nature of matter and energy. The equation states that energy (E) and mass (m) are interchangeable and related to each other by the speed of light (c) squared. This means that a small amount of mass can be transformed into a huge amount of energy, and vice versa.

The theory has far-reaching implications, and it has been confirmed by numerous experiments and observations. It is the basis for our understanding of nuclear reactions, including both the power sources in nuclear reactors and the destructive weapons of nuclear bombs. It also provides a way of understanding how matter and energy are created and destroyed in the universe, and how they are related to each other in the most fundamental way.

The theory was first proposed by Albert Einstein in 1905 and is based on the idea that the laws of physics should be the same for all observers, regardless of their relative motion. This idea, known as the theory of special relativity, was revolutionary at the time and challenged many of the prevailing ideas about the nature of space and time.

E=mc^2 is a relatively simple equation, but its implications are far-reaching and profound. It provides a way of understanding the fundamental relationship between matter and energy, and how the energy content of an object is directly related to its mass. It also shows that a small amount of matter can be transformed into an enormous amount of energy, a concept that has been put to use in the development of nuclear reactors and weapons.

Einstein's theory of mass-energy equivalence is a landmark in the history of physics, and its impact continues to be felt in many areas of science and technology. Whether you're a scientist, engineer, or simply curious about the world around you, E=mc^2 is a concept that is well worth exploring.

In Path Bender, the concept of energy and matter are considered to be interconnected and interdependent. The teachings emphasize the idea that all things, including matter, are made up of energy, and that this energy can be transformed into matter and vice versa.

This concept aligns with Einstein's famous equation, $E=mc^2$, which states that energy (E) is equal to mass (m) multiplied by the speed of light (c) squared. This equation demonstrates that energy and matter are interchangeable and that energy can be transformed into matter and vice versa.

The relationship between energy and matter in Path Bender's teachings can be compared to the relationship between energy and matter in Einstein's theory. Just as Path Bender's teachings emphasize the idea that all things are made up of energy, Einstein's equation demonstrates that matter is simply a form of energy. And just as Path Bender's teachings emphasize the idea that energy can be transformed into matter, Einstein's equation demonstrates that energy can be transformed into matter through the relationship between energy, mass, and the speed of light.

In Path Bender, the concept of energy transformation is central to spiritual growth and development. Just as energy can be transformed into matter, individuals can transform their own energy and consciousness to achieve greater awareness and understanding. This idea aligns with

Einstein's theory, as the transformation of energy into matter is central to the understanding of the physical universe and the nature of reality.

Path Bender's teachings and Einstein's theory of E=mc^2 are both based on the idea that energy and matter are interconnected and interdependent. Both emphasize the idea that energy can be transformed into matter, and that this transformation is central to our understanding of the universe and our own spiritual growth and development.

The Nature of Mass: Understanding Inertia in Physical Objects

Mass is a fundamental concept in physics and it refers to the amount of matter in a physical body. It determines the object's resistance to changes in its motion, or what we call its inertia. Simply put, the greater the mass of an object, the greater its resistance to motion and change.

One of the most important features of mass is that it is always conserved in a physical system. This means that the total amount of mass in a closed system will always remain constant, regardless of the changes that take place within that system.

Inertia is directly proportional to mass, as stated by Newton's first law of motion. It states that an object at rest will remain at rest and an object in motion will continue to move at a constant velocity unless acted upon by an unbalanced force. This means that the greater the mass of an object, the greater the force required to change its velocity.

This is why it is more difficult to change the velocity of a heavy object than a lighter one. For example, consider a small ball and a bowling ball. It is much easier to throw the small ball than the bowling ball because the bowling ball has a greater mass and thus a greater inertia.

It's important to understand the relationship between mass and inertia because it plays a critical role in our understanding of the physical world around us. From everyday experiences to complex scientific experiments, the principles of mass and inertia play a fundamental role in shaping our understanding of the universe.

Mass is the quantity of matter in a physical body and determines its inertia. It is a fundamental concept in physics and plays a critical role in shaping our understanding of the physical world. Understanding the relationship between mass and inertia helps us make predictions about how objects will behave and respond to forces, and is an essential part of our understanding of the universe.

The Intersection of Mass, Inertia, and Path Bender's Thoughts and Emotions Become Creations

Mass and inertia are two fundamental concepts in physics that have long been studied and understood by scientists. Mass, as defined by physics, is the quantity of matter in a body that determines its resistance to change in motion.

Inertia, on the other hand, is the property of matter that allows it to resist any change in motion. These concepts form the foundation of classical mechanics and have been used to explain the behavior of objects in the physical world.

However, the philosophy of Path Bender's teachings suggests that thoughts and emotions also play a significant role in determining the experiences we have in life. According to this philosophy, thoughts and emotions are not just abstract concepts but are tangible, real-world creations that shape our reality.

Just as mass and inertia govern the behavior of physical matter, thoughts and emotions shape our experiences, thoughts and emotions become creations.

In light of this philosophy, the concepts of mass and inertia can be viewed from a different perspective. Mass can be seen as the accumulation of thoughts and emotions that have been generated over time. Inertia, on the other hand, can be seen as the resistance of our thoughts and emotions to change. Just as physical matter resists any change in motion, our thoughts and emotions also tend to persist and maintain their momentum, shaping our reality in the process.

Thus, the interplay between mass, inertia, and thoughts and emotions is central to the philosophy of Path Bender's teachings. Our thoughts and emotions, just like mass, accumulate over time and determine our reality. Inertia, on the other hand, determines the persistence of our thoughts and emotions, shaping our experiences and the world around us.

The relationship between mass, inertia, and Path Bender's philosophy of thoughts and emotions becoming creations provides us with a new perspective on the nature of reality. It suggests that our thoughts and emotions play a significant role in shaping our reality, just as physical matter is shaped by its mass and inertia. Understanding this relationship can help us to better understand the nature of our experiences and create a more positive and fulfilling reality.

Manifesting Reality: The Interplay of Thoughts, Emotions, Mass and Inertia in Path Bender Philosophy

It is said in Path Bender teachings that Thoughts and Emotions become Creations, meaning that our internal mental and emotional state directly affects the manifestation of our reality. In this sense, mass and inertia can be seen as powerful physical representations of our inner thoughts and emotions.

Mass, as defined by physics, is the quantity of matter in a body and determines its inertia, or resistance to change. In other words, the more mass an object has, the more difficult it is to alter its state of motion. This concept can be applied to our own thoughts and emotions. Just like physical objects, our mental and emotional state also has mass, and similarly, this mass accumulates over time, becoming more and more difficult to change.

However, Path Bender teachings go beyond the physical understanding of mass and inertia. In this philosophy, thoughts and emotions are not just passive states, but active forces that shape our reality. By harnessing the power of our thoughts and emotions, Path Benders are able to overcome the inertia of their mental and emotional state, and consciously manifest their reality.

The Interplay of Thoughts, Emotions, and Manifestation: A Path Bender Perspective

In this way, mass and inertia are integral parts of the manifestation process of a Path Bender. The more mass our thoughts and emotions have, the more resistance they have to change, but through the practice of mindfulness and intention, Path Benders are able to change the direction of their thoughts and emotions, and thus alter their reality.

The interplay between mass, inertia, and thoughts and emotions is a central aspect of the philosophy of Path Bender's teachings. By understanding and harnessing the power of these forces, Path Benders are able to bring their deepest desires and intentions into reality.

In the Path Bender philosophy, the relationship between force, acceleration, mass, and thoughts and emotions is a critical aspect of the manifestation process. Thoughts are considered to be the equivalent of force, while emotions are seen as the equivalent of acceleration. When these two elements interact, they create mass, which serves as the foundation for manifestation.

To understand this process, it is important to first recognize the power of thoughts and emotions. Thoughts and emotions are not just abstract concepts, but are energy forms that exist within us and influence the world around us. They shape our perceptions, create our experiences, and determine the nature of our reality.

In this sense, thoughts can be seen as the force that drives our experiences and emotions, while acceleration represents the rate at which these experiences are shaping our reality. Just as a force acting upon an object will cause it to accelerate, our thoughts and emotions will also create momentum, shaping the course of our lives and the world around us.

The accumulation of thoughts and emotions over time gives rise to mass, which serves as the basis for manifestation. In the Path Bender philosophy, this mass is not just a physical quantity, but is seen as a manifestation of our thoughts and emotions. In other words, it is the physical manifestation of our thoughts and emotions that we experience as reality.

Therefore, in the Path Bender philosophy, the interplay between thoughts, emotions, and manifestation is a critical aspect of the manifestation process. By aligning our thoughts and emotions with our goals and intentions, we can create the mass necessary to bring our desires into being. The more focused and intentional our thoughts and emotions are, the more powerful our manifestation will be.

The Path Bender philosophy views the relationship between force, acceleration, mass, and thoughts and emotions as an integral part of the manifestation process. By understanding the power of our thoughts and emotions and using them to create mass, we can shape our reality and bring our desires into being.

CHAPTER 18: SHAPING YOUR REALITY

The Transformative Power of Thought Energy

In the philosophy of Path Benders, thoughts hold immense power as they are the driving force behind our reality. The principle of the conservation of energy states that energy can neither be created nor destroyed, it can only be transformed from one form to another. Similarly, thought energy follows the same principle. Our thoughts cannot be created or destroyed, but they can be transformed into a different form. This is where the concept of "thought energy becoming manifest" comes into play.

The process of manifestation begins with our thoughts, which are considered to be a form of energy. Our thoughts hold the potential to influence our emotions, which are also considered to be a form of energy. As our thoughts and emotions accumulate, they have the potential to create mass. The accumulation of thought and emotional energy is like a force that exerts its influence on our reality, shaping it in a specific way.

In order to bend our reality towards our desired outcomes, we must learn to control our thoughts and emotions. This is where the concept of "thought acceleration" comes into play. Our thoughts and emotions must be directed in a specific direction with a specific intention. This direction and intention give our thoughts and emotions the necessary acceleration to create the desired manifestation.

It is important to understand that we cannot create thought energy, but we can transform it into something that serves our dreams. Our thoughts and emotions are like a force that has the potential to shape our reality. We must learn to harness this force, directing it towards our desired outcome, to manifest our dreams into reality.

The transformative power of thought energy is at the heart of Path Bender philosophy. Our thoughts and emotions hold immense potential, which must be directed towards our desired outcomes. By learning to control our thoughts and emotions, we can bend our reality towards our desired manifestation, transforming thought energy into a force that serves our dreams.

A Journey of Motherhood in a Futuristic Society

In the year 5000, the world was a vastly different place. The great Crisis of 3500 had ravaged the planet, leaving behind only a handful of giant domed cities as the last bastions of human civilization. The people of these cities were ruled by two unbreakable laws - strict adherence to Life Quality, and a complete ban on reproduction, with only the "worthy" being allowed to bring new life into the world.

This was the world that Aria lived in. She was a young woman with a passion for technology and a curious mind, always exploring the limits of what was possible. It was in one of her expeditions that she stumbled upon a mysterious device that would change her life forever.

One day, as she was exploring the remnants of an ancient society, she stumbled upon a strange object. It was a small, sleek device, unlike anything she had ever seen before. Despite her curiosity, Aria was initially hesitant to touch it, but she was drawn to it all the same. As she reached out to pick it up, she was suddenly bathed in a warm, comforting light.

In that moment, Aria's entire world changed. She felt a rush of positive energy coursing through her veins, filling her with confidence and happiness. The device, it turned out, was a mind-altering device, capable of transforming negative thoughts into positive ones.

Overwhelmed by her newfound sense of hope, Aria quickly realized that this was the key to unlocking a brighter future for herself and for humanity. With this new device, people would be able to shed their limiting beliefs and negative thoughts, freeing themselves from the constraints of the past and embracing a brighter, more hopeful future.

Aria soon discovered that she had been selected to reproduce, a rare and highly coveted honor in her society. But despite her newfound confidence and hope, Aria was not interested in being a mother. Instead, she set her sights on a much larger goal - to share the knowledge of this device with the people of her city, so that they too could transform their lives and their world.

With a newfound sense of purpose, Aria began her mission to spread the word of the mind-altering device, traveling from city to city, sharing her story and inspiring others to take control of their thoughts and their lives. The people of the domed cities were skeptical at first, but as Aria's message spread, more and more people began to embrace the idea of change, of shedding their negative thoughts and beliefs, and of creating a better world for themselves and for future generations.

And so, Aria's legacy lived on, as people all over the world embraced the power of positive thoughts, and worked together to build a brighter, more hopeful future for all.

The Principle of Sowing and Reaping in Path Bender Philosophy

Path Benders understand the power of their thoughts and emotions and their impact on their reality. With this knowledge comes the responsibility of respecting the principle of sowing and reaping. This principle states that what we put out into the world, whether it be thoughts or actions, will come back to us in some form. In other words, we reap what we sow.

This principle is a key component of Path Bender teachings and is taken very seriously. Path Benders believe that their thoughts and emotions carry energy and that this energy is constantly shaping their reality. With this in mind, they make a conscious effort to focus their thoughts and emotions on positivity and love.

However, Path Benders also understand that sometimes their thoughts and emotions may not align with their desired reality. This is why they make a conscious effort to change their thoughts and emotions, so they can attract the experiences and outcomes they desire.

In addition to their thoughts and emotions, Path Benders also understand the power of their actions. They believe that every action they take, no matter how small, has a ripple effect on their reality. This is why Path Benders are very careful of the actions they do unto others. They understand that those actions, or seeds sown into the ground, will eventually come back to them in some form.

The principle of sowing and reaping is a reminder to Path Benders to be mindful of their thoughts, emotions, and actions. They understand that their reality is a reflection of their inner world, and they make a conscious effort to cultivate a positive inner world. In doing so, they attract positive experiences and outcomes into their lives.

The principle of sowing and reaping is a fundamental part of Path Bender philosophy. Path Benders respect and live by this principle, understanding that their thoughts, emotions, and actions have a profound impact on their reality. By taking responsibility for their thoughts and actions, Path Benders are able to shape their reality and manifest their desired experiences and outcomes.

The Principle of Multiplication

As Path Benders, we understand the importance of the principle of multiplication. This principle states that we will always reap more than we sow, and we take this principle very seriously. Whether it's our thoughts, emotions, actions, or even products, we aim to sow positive energy and good deeds into the world and reap the rewards of our efforts.

However, we also recognize that this principle works in reverse. When we act negatively or treat others poorly, the same principle applies, and we will receive the negative consequences of our actions. This is why Path Benders are so careful about the actions they do unto others, as they understand the impact it will have on their own lives and realities.

In business, for example, Path Benders take full advantage of the principle of multiplication by providing top-notch customer service, creating high-quality products, and treating their employees with respect and fairness. These actions not only improve the lives of those around them, but also bring great rewards and success to the Path Bender.

On the flip side, Path Benders are mindful of the negative impact they can have, and they work to minimize it. They understand that it's important to consider the consequences of their actions, not just for themselves but for those around them. They aim to create positive energy, not negative, and to sow kindness and generosity into the world.

The principle of multiplication is a powerful tool that Path Benders use to manifest their desires and realities. Whether it's in their personal or professional lives, they aim to reap the rewards of their positive actions, while being mindful of the negative consequences that can come from their negative actions. By embracing this principle, Path Benders strive to create a world of abundance and positivity.

The Seeds of Change: A Tale of Love, Loss, and Growth

Once upon a time, there was a young woman named Amelia who lived a simple and contented life. She had a passion for gardening and loved to spend her days tending to her flowers and vegetables. One day, she met a young man named Liam who swept her off her feet. They fell deeply in love and before she knew it, Liam proposed to her. Amelia was over the moon and couldn't imagine a happier life with her soulmate by her side.

However, things took a turn for the worse when Liam suddenly ended their relationship without any explanation. Amelia was crushed and didn't understand what went wrong. She found solace in the words of Dakota Fanning's character in Uptown Girls, "In life every ending is just a new beginning." She took comfort in the idea that maybe this break-up was just the start of something even better.

As she continued to tend to her garden, she noticed that the same principles applied to her life as they did to her plants. Just as she had to sow the seeds, water and care for them, so too did she have to take care of herself, both physically and emotionally. As she began to focus on her own well-being, she realized that she had been holding herself back from reaching her full potential. She started to take action towards her goals and before she knew it, she was on a path of self-discovery and growth.

Meanwhile, Liam was struggling with his own fears and insecurities. He was a talented young man, but he was afraid that his fear of failure would hold him back from achieving his full potential. As he took a closer look at his life, he realized that his fear was keeping him from taking risks and pursuing his dreams. He decided that he needed to face his fears head on and started to take action towards his goals.

As fate would have it, Amelia and Liam eventually crossed paths again. They both saw how much the other had grown and were amazed at the positive changes they had made in their lives. They reconnected and started a new relationship, stronger and more confident than ever before. They learned that endings can be tough, but they can also be a chance for new beginnings and growth. And just as the seeds they sowed in their garden flourished, so too did their relationship blossom into something beautiful.

The end.

Life is a Reflection of Your Thoughts

The human mind is a powerful tool that can shape our lives in countless ways. Our thoughts, beliefs, and attitudes have a direct impact on our daily experiences, and the way we see the world around us. It is often said that our thoughts create our reality, and this statement is not far from the truth. Our dominant thoughts are the foundation upon which we build our lives, and they determine the type of experiences we have on a daily basis.

One's thoughts are the result of their beliefs, and beliefs are the result of their experiences. When we repeatedly think the same thoughts, they become deeply ingrained in our subconscious mind and become our automatic thought patterns. These dominant thoughts then shape our perceptions, attitudes, and beliefs, and they influence the decisions we make and the actions we take. This is why it is so important to be mindful of our thoughts, and to take control of them, instead of allowing them to control us.

The way we think about ourselves and the world around us has a profound effect on our lives. When we have positive and optimistic thoughts, we feel confident, energized, and motivated. We see the world as a place full of opportunities and possibilities, and we are more likely to take risks, pursue our goals, and experience success. On the other hand, when we have negative and pessimistic thoughts, we feel discouraged, defeated, and unmotivated. We see the world as a place full of obstacles and challenges, and we are less likely to take action, pursue our goals, and experience success.

It is important to note that our thoughts are not just a reflection of our experiences, they are also a reflection of our beliefs and attitudes. Our beliefs and attitudes determine how we respond to the challenges and opportunities that life presents to us. They influence our thoughts, and in turn, our thoughts influence our beliefs and attitudes. This creates a feedback loop that shapes our perceptions of reality and determines the type of life we lead.

Therefore, if you want to improve your life, you must start by improving your thoughts. You must be mindful of the dominant thoughts that run through your mind, and you must learn to replace negative and limiting thoughts with positive and empowering ones. This requires discipline and consistency, but it is a crucial step towards creating a life that you love.

Your life is a reflection of your dominant thoughts. Your thoughts, beliefs, and attitudes determine the type of experiences you have, and they shape the world around you. By taking control of your thoughts, and replacing negative and limiting thoughts with positive and empowering ones, you can create a life that is full of joy, abundance, and success. Remember, your thoughts have the power to shape your reality, so choose them wisely.

The Power of Changing Limiting Beliefs and Your Story

Every person has a unique story that they tell themselves and others, but often these stories are not only a representation of their experiences, but also the beliefs they hold about themselves and the world. These beliefs can limit the opportunities available to them and shape the way they perceive reality.

Limiting beliefs can take many forms, such as beliefs about oneself being not good enough, not deserving success or happiness, or not being capable of change. These limiting beliefs can be so deeply ingrained in a person's mind that they become a self-fulfilling prophecy, limiting their potential and holding them back from reaching their goals.

It is therefore crucial to change these limiting beliefs and the story one tells themselves and others. This can be done by becoming aware of the negative thoughts and beliefs that are holding one back, and reframing them into positive, empowering beliefs. This process involves challenging the negative beliefs and replacing them with a new story that aligns with one's values and goals.

One important aspect of changing limiting beliefs is self-reflection. By taking the time to understand one's thought patterns and beliefs, they can start to see how they shape their experiences and their reality. This understanding can lead to a shift in perspective and a newfound confidence in one's ability to change their thoughts and beliefs.

Another important aspect of changing limiting beliefs is seeking out new experiences that challenge the limiting beliefs. By taking risks and stepping outside of one's comfort zone, one can demonstrate to themselves that their limiting beliefs are not absolute truths, but rather just a story they have been telling themselves.

Finally, it is important to seek support from others. Surrounding oneself with positive, supportive people who believe in them can help to reinforce the new, empowering beliefs and reinforce the change in one's story.

Changing limiting beliefs and the story one tells themselves and others can have a profound impact on their life. By becoming aware of the negative thoughts and beliefs that are holding them back, reframing them into positive, empowering beliefs, seeking new experiences that challenge the limiting beliefs, and seeking support from others, one can transform their life and reach their full potential.

CHAPTER 19: THE AWAKENING

As Sarah sat in her dimly lit room, surrounded by the remnants of heartbreak and disappointment, Sarah couldn't help but feel lost and hopeless. The pain of her fiancé breaking up with her was like a knife in her chest, and she couldn't seem to shake it off.

Just as she was about to lose all hope, she stumbled upon a video of a motivational speaker named John, who spoke about the power of energy and the infinite potential of the human spirit. She was immediately drawn in by his words and found herself watching video after video of him.

One particular quote from John stuck with her: "You are not a finite body, you are an energy field." Sarah couldn't help but wonder what that meant. She had always defined herself by her physical form and her accomplishments, but could there be something more to her existence?

Determined to find out, Sarah decided to attend one of John's live events. The energy in the room was electric as John spoke about the infinite power of the human spirit and the connection between all things in the universe. Sarah felt as though she was experiencing a spiritual awakening, and she realized that the love she had been seeking was within her all along.

John's words resonated with Sarah, and she realized that she had the power to create the life she wanted. She no longer wanted to be defined by her past heartbreak and disappointment, but rather by her own limitless potential. She was filled with a newfound sense of purpose and determination, and she was ready to harness the power of her energy to create a life worthy of her.

Contemplating the words she had just heard. She was shocked to realize that she had been defining herself by her finite body, but in reality, she was so much more. She was an energy field, an extension of Source energy, and she had the potential and power to create her world as she wanted it to be.

She had always thought that her life was determined by circumstances and external factors, but now she saw that she was the one who held the power to change her reality. Her thoughts, her beliefs, and her emotions were all energies that were shaping her reality.

She began to understand that her life experiences were a reflection of her own beliefs, and if she wanted different results, she needed to change her beliefs. The first step was to be aware of the thoughts she was thinking and the stories she was telling herself.

She closed her eyes and took a deep breath, feeling the energy within her. She imagined herself being connected to the infinite field of unfolding possibility, and she let go of her limiting beliefs and fears. She felt a rush of energy and excitement, and she knew that she had the power to create a new reality for herself.

She opened her eyes, feeling refreshed and empowered. She knew that it wouldn't be easy, but she was ready to take on the challenge and become the master of her own destiny. She was no longer a victim of her circumstances, but a powerful being who had the ability to bend the path of her life in any direction she chose.

She stood up, feeling lighter and more confident. She took one step forward, and then another, and she knew that she was on her way to a brighter future, one that was worthy of her and full of love, joy, and abundance.

As Sarah reflected on the power she held within herself, she couldn't help but think about how she had been living her life up until now. She had been constantly seeking external validation and trying to fit in with .

those around her. But now, she realized that her true power lay within her own thoughts and beliefs.

She remembered the words of the wise teacher, that she was a spiritual being, an extension of Source energy, and had the potential to create her own world. This realization filled her with a newfound sense of purpose and excitement.

Sarah knew that she could no longer waste her time seeking approval from others or living a life that was not aligned with her true desires. She was determined to harness the power within her and create a life that was worthy of her infinite potential.

With this newfound understanding, Sarah closed her eyes and began to meditate. She focused on her breath and visualized the life she truly desired. She saw herself living in a beautiful home surrounded by love and happiness. She saw herself traveling the world, experiencing new cultures, and making a positive impact on those around her.

As she held this vision in her mind, Sarah felt a sense of peace and contentment wash over her. She knew that this was just the beginning of her journey, but she was ready to embrace it with open arms. She was ready to become a Path Bender, to harness the power within her and create the life she truly desired.

And so, with a smile on her face and a sense of hope in her heart, Sarah opened her eyes and stepped forward, ready to bend her path and shape her destiny.

As Sarah pondered on the concept of energy and her true nature, she began to feel a sense of liberation. For so long, she had defined herself by her body and her physical limitations, but now she understood that she was so much more. She was an extension of Source energy, with the power to create and shape her reality.

She thought back on the events of her life, and the results she had been experiencing. She realized that many of her fears and limitations had been holding her back from achieving her true potential. She was in control of her life and had the power to create a reality that was truly worthy of her.

So, she decided to make a change. She started to focus her thoughts and energy on what she truly wanted in life. She visualized her desired outcomes and spoke them into existence. She realized that the world was not against her, but instead, she was the one holding herself back.

As Sarah continued to practice this new way of thinking and being, she began to see incredible changes in her life. Opportunities and relationships that she never thought were possible started to unfold before her. She felt a newfound sense of confidence and empowerment, and she finally felt that she was living in alignment with her true nature.

Sarah had discovered the power of sowing and reaping. She understood that the energy she put out into the world was reflected back to her in the form of her experiences. She was no longer a victim of her circumstances, but instead, was the master of her own destiny.

From that day on, Sarah lived a life that was truly worthy of her. She illuminated her city, not with her body's potential, but with the unlimited power of her spirit. She was a path bender, and nothing could stop her from creating a life that was filled with love, joy, and abundance.

We Are Path Benders

We are the creators of our own experience, and the law of attraction is at our disposal. We have the power to deliberately guide our thoughts and emotions towards a feeling tone of harmony and happiness, and this is where the law of attraction starts to respond. This means we can shift our beliefs and attitudes towards life and start seeing things in a positive light. We can break free from old patterns and societal beliefs and prove that the power within us is greater than anything in the world.

We encourage you to take control of your thoughts and beliefs, to imagine the world you want to live in and to focus on that world. When we focus on what we want, what we don't want simply falls away.

So, ask yourself: what do you choose now? The real "what" is, what are you going to do with your thoughts and beliefs from this moment forward? The power is in your hands.

Our thoughts shape our lives and reminds us that we have the power to create the life we want. By focusing on what we want and guiding our thoughts and emotions, we can use the law of attraction to manifest our desires and live a life filled with harmony, happiness, and abundance.

Embracing Your Limitless Potential

As we come to the end of our journey in Path Bender, it is important to reflect on what we have learned and how we can apply these lessons to our lives. We have explored the power of our thoughts and how they shape our reality. We have discovered the importance of focusing on what we want instead of what we don't want. And we have learned about the law of attraction and how it can help us create the life we desire.

But for many of us, there may be a voice of doubt that whispers, "I can't do that." We may think that we are not strong enough, rich enough, or smart enough to achieve our dreams. This is a common belief that holds many people back from reaching their full potential.

The truth is that we are unlimited beings. We have no ceiling and no limits to what we can achieve. There is no blackboard in the sky that dictates our purpose or mission in life. Our purpose is what we say it is, and our mission is the mission we give ourselves.

Neale Donald Walsch learned this lesson when he realized that his primary aim in life was to feel and experience joy. He began to do only those things that brought him joy and happiness, and he encourages us to do the same. If it doesn't bring us joy, then it is not worth doing.

It is time for us to embrace our limitless potential and to live our lives to the fullest. It is time for us to release our fears and limitations and to trust in our ability to create the life we want. It is time for us to take control of our thoughts, to focus on what we want, and to trust in the law of attraction to bring us the abundance and happiness that we deserve.

So, as we bring Path Bender to a close, we encourage you to embrace your limitless potential, to live your life with joy and purpose, and to never give up on your dreams. The power to create the life you want is within you, and the universe is waiting to respond to your every thought and desire.

Bend Your Path With Us

The journey of life is about finding happiness, love, freedom, and joy. These are the things that make life worth living, and the things that should drive us every day. Many of us grow up with the belief that there is a specific purpose or mission that we must fulfill in life, but the truth is, your purpose and mission are what you make of them. The key to a fulfilling life is to focus on what makes you feel good, and to pursue that with all your heart.

Inner happiness is the fuel of success. When you are in a state of joy and contentment, your thoughts and intentions are more powerful, and you will attract more of what you want into your life. It doesn't matter what brings you joy - be it meditation, spending time with loved ones, or eating your favorite sandwich - what's important is that you put yourself in that state as often as possible.

Joseph Campbell once said, "Follow your bliss." This is sage advice, as when you follow your passions and the things that bring you joy, you will naturally attract abundance and well-being into your life. This is the path that we invite you to follow with us.

As you read this book, you are making a choice to take control of your life and to bend your path in the direction of happiness and fulfillment. We believe that life is phenomenal, and that it should be enjoyed to the fullest. Join us on this journey, and let's experience all the wonders that this world has to offer.

Embrace Your Bliss

As we come to the end of our journey in Path Bender, I hope that you have gained a deeper understanding of the unlimited potential that lies within each and every one of us. The choice is ours to harness that potential, to embrace our bliss and to follow the trail to abundance and well-being on all subjects.

Joseph Campbell's words, "Follow your bliss," are a powerful reminder of the importance of listening to our hearts and pursuing what brings us joy and fulfillment. When we align ourselves with our passions and desires, we tap into a boundless source of energy and creativity that can lead us to a life beyond our wildest dreams.

The path to this life of abundance and well-being is yours to forge. It's a journey that requires courage, perseverance, and a willingness to let go of what no longer serves us. But the reward is a life filled with joy, love, freedom, happiness, and laughter.

As we move into this new era of unbounded potential and possibilities, we invite you to join us on the path to discovery. Embrace your bliss and live a life that is truly phenomenal. I thank you for choosing to bend your path with us. May your journey be filled with love, light, and endless possibility.

A Final Message From Antonio

And let that be the guiding principle of your life, to follow your bliss and to do what makes your heart sing. Let that be the foundation upon which you build your reality, for the possibilities are truly endless.

The power of your mind is vast, and it is capable of shaping the world around you in ways you cannot imagine. So dream big, and let your imagination soar. Remember, the only limits are the ones you place upon yourself. And with the knowledge you have gained through Path Bender, you now have the tools to break free from those self-imposed limitations.

So go forth, my friend, and create a life that is filled with love, joy, and abundance. Let your light shine bright and be an inspiration to those around you. And always remember, the journey is just as important as the destination. So enjoy the trip, for life is truly phenomenal.

And to those who will one day follow in your footsteps, may they be inspired by your journey and find the courage to follow their own path, to bend their own path, and to create a life that is rich and fulfilling in every way. For this is the power of the human spirit, and this is the promise of a brighter tomorrow.

So here's to you, my friend. May your life be filled with love, happiness, and all the things that you desire. May you find the courage to follow your own path, and may your journey be filled with wonder and delight. You are the master of your own destiny, and you have the power to create the life of your dreams. So go forth, and live your life to the fullest!

And so, we come to the end of Path Bender, a journey of self-discovery and personal growth. We have explored my creation of Path Bender's and the power within each of us that is greater than the world. This power has the ability to shape our thoughts and influence our experiences, and it is available to us at all times, no matter how old or young we might be.

The moment we began to think properly, this power within us becomes accessible. It is the spark that ignites the fire of our desires and passions. It is the fuel that drives us forward, towards a life filled with abundance, well-being, and joy.

As you close the pages of this book, remember that the power within you is waiting to be unlocked. Embrace it, harness it, and allow it to guide you towards your dreams. Remember that you are the creator of your own life, and that anything is possible.

So go forth, with confidence and purpose, knowing that you have the power to shape your own reality. And never forget, there is a powerful Path Bender inside of you, guiding and supporting you, every step of the way. I love you, even though I never met you.

And finally, know that you are not alone. My life extends far beyond the limitations of myself, just as yours does. We are all connected, all a part of the same beautiful, boundless universe. So let us continue to walk this path together, supporting each other, lifting each other up, and transcending the boundaries that once held us back.

All is well. All is perfectly, damnably well.

Best,

Antonio T Smith Jr.

Thank you for buying this book.

Are you an Antonio T Smith Jr fan? Join him on social media. He would love to hear from you!

OFFICIAL FACEBOOK PAGE:

https://www.facebook.com/theatsjr

FACEBOOK FAN CLUB:

https://www.facebook.com/groups/theofficialantoniotsmithjrfanclub

AUTHOR WEBSITE:

Books.AntonioTSmithJr.com

CATCH ME ON TOUR:

https://antoniotsmithjr.com/

INSTAGRAM:

instagram.com/theatsjr

EMAIL: books@antoniotsmithjr.com

CPSIA information can be obtained
at www.ICGtesting.com
Printed in the USA
BVHW051020270223
659295BV00014B/441/J